User Guide for
Getting AHEAD
while Getting Out

A prisoner reentry model to reduce recidivism through learning, building resources, accountability, and collaboration

DeVol, Philip E.; Wood, Michelle R.; Libster, Mitchell A.
   User Guide for Getting Ahead while Getting Out: A prisoner reentry model to reduce recidivism through learning, building resources, accountability, and collaboration

198 pp.
Bibliography: pp. 165–171
ISBN: 978-1-938248-57-3

© 2015 by DeVol & Associates, LLC
Published by aha! Process, Inc.

All rights reserved. Printed in the United States of America. No part of this book may be reproduced in any manner whatsoever without written permission, except in the case of brief quotations embedded in critical articles and reviews. For information, address aha! Process, Inc., P.O. Box 727, Highlands, TX 77562-0727; fax (281) 426-5600; *www.ahaprocess.com*

Book design by Paula Nicolella
Illustrations by Scott Knauer
Copy editing by Dan Shenk

Other titles by Philip E. DeVol (published by aha! Process, Inc. unless otherwise indicated):

Getting Ahead in a Just-Gettin'-By World (2004, 2013)
   Philip E. DeVol

Facilitator Notes for Getting Ahead in a Just-Gettin'-By World (2004, 2013)
   Philip E. DeVol

Two-book set for colleges adapted from *Getting Ahead in a Just-Gettin'-By World:*

   Investigations into Economic Class in America (2010)
      Philip E. DeVol and Karla M. Krodel

   Facilitator Notes for Investigations into Economic Class in America (2010)
      Philip E. DeVol and Karla M. Krodel

Bridges Out of Poverty: Strategies for Professionals and Communities (1999, 2009)
   Ruby K. Payne, PhD, Philip E. DeVol, and Terie Dreussi-Smith

Bridges to Sustainable Communities: A Systemwide, Cradle-to-Grave Approach to Ending Poverty in America (2010)
   Philip E. DeVol

The Complete Guide to Elementary Student Assistance Programs: Strategy, Policy, and Procedure (1993)
   Linda Christensen and Philip E. DeVol (Center City, MN: Hazelden Educational Materials)

User Guide for Getting AHEAD while Getting Out

A prisoner reentry model to reduce recidivism through learning, building resources, accountability, and collaboration

Philip E. DeVol, Michelle R. Wood, and Mitchell A. Libster

Table of Contents

Acknowledgments	vii
Message from the Authors	ix
Getting Ahead: What It's About	1
a. Overview	1
b. Philosophy of Getting Ahead	2
c. Description: The 'Kitchen Table' Learning Experience	4
d. The Process: How It Works	6
e. How to Provide Getting Ahead while Getting Out Inside Correctional Facilities	16
f. Two Accountability Charts	17
g. Getting Out Reentry Model	22
h. Frequently Asked Questions About the Reentry Model	25
i. Data Collection, Evaluations, Reports, and Social Media	28
j. How Getting Out Fits into Bridges Initiatives	33
k. The Community	33
l. Support from aha! Process	35
Support for GA Graduates	39
a. Investigators' Initiatives—Support for Each Other	40
b. Community Models That Benefit GA Graduates	44
c. Institutional and Sector Approaches That Benefit GA Graduates	45
Support for Facilitators and Co-Facilitators	53
a. Facilitator Knowledge, Skills, and Attitude	53
b. Patterns in the *Getting Out* Workbook	54
c. Knowledge of Oneself as a Facilitator	55
d. Continuous Learning	56
e. Things to Know: Michelle's Hidden Rules of Prison Life	56
f. Things Facilitators Need to Know About Working with Offenders	56
g. Things to Know About Working with Returning Citizens	57
h. Things to Know About Working with Correctional Staff	57
i. Things to Know About Working with Adults	58
j. Information About Groups	58
k. Suggested Schedule of Modules per Session	59
l. Tips for Running the Group	60
m. Support from Getting Ahead Network	64

Module-by-Module Instructions	**69**
Module 1: My Life upon Release	71
Module 2: The Importance of Language	77
Module 3: Theory of Change	83
Module 4: The Rich/Poor Gap and Research on Causes of Poverty	91
Module 5: Hidden Rules of Economic Class	107
Module 6: Eleven Resources	117
Module 7: Threat Assessment	121
Module 8: Self-Assessment of Resources	123
Module 9: Community Assessment	127
Module 10: Building Resources	133
Module 11: Personal and Community Plans	137
Appendix	**141**
1. Sequence and Reinforcement of Key Concepts Found in Getting Ahead	142
2. Getting Ahead—the Purpose of Each Module	151
3. Model Fidelity Elements for Conducting the Getting Ahead Workshop	155
4. Activity: Newspapers and Magazines—Understanding How Economic Disparity Affects Us Concretely and Abstractly	156
5. Sustainable Communities Where Everyone Can Live Well	157
6. Maslow's Hierarchy of Needs	159
7. Data Collection, Evaluations, Research, and Social Capital	160
8. Websites	161
9. Glossary of Terms Used in Corrections and This *User Guide*	162
Bibliography	**165**
Index	**173**
About the Authors	**183**

Acknowledgments

Getting Ahead™ graduates constantly push the envelope of learning. Hardly a day goes by that someone isn't lighting up the computer screen or phone lines with new ideas and deeper, more relevant applications of our work. This was true when developing the 2013 edition of *Facilitator Notes for Getting Ahead in a Just-Gettin'-By World,* and it's true in this adaptation titled *User Guide for Getting Ahead while Getting Out,* which is designed primarily for people who are returning to their communities from correctional facilities and jails.

First we want to acknowledge the contributions of the men who were in Getting Ahead (GA) groups from the Reintegration Camp at the Marion Correctional Institution (MCI) in Marion, OH. The following men shared their reactions, ideas, and wisdom about every module in this book. Some men wrote papers for our education with the intention of making this book really work for returning citizens: Mitch Alberty, Raymond Allen, James Bell, Cory Bowden, John Brown, Jesús Chavez, David Dillinger, Tony Eckard, Thomas Fout, Thomas Harris, Joshua Higgins, Raymond Hudnall, Doug Hunt, Tim Jones, Jason Kilgour, Troy Koon, James Kouger, Gilbert Martinez, Terrance Mason, Joshua Radar, and Todd Stapleton. Special thanks to Mark Merriweather and Robert Minniefield, Getting Ahead graduates and co-facilitators.

We were assisted by Phil Townsend and Jeannie Brewer, who facilitated groups at MCI and provided their insights to us about the content and process of GA.

There is a broader learning community of Bridges Out of Poverty trainers and Getting Ahead facilitator across the U.S. and other countries. We would like to thank Elain Ellerbe, Rochelle Johns, and Mickie Lewis who also advised us on both this workbook and the *User Guide*.

It was extremely valuable for the authors to learn from people working in the criminal justice system and the correctional facilities. We were guided by Warden Jason Bunting, Unit Manager Martha Jerew, and Unit Manager Pamela Shaw. Organizations that provided support are the Mid-Ohio Reentry Coalition, Marion Matters, and the Marion Branch of the Legal Aid Society of Columbus where co-authors Mitchell Libster and Michelle Wood were employed.

We also would like to thank the following: Jody Demo-Hodgins with the Crawford-Marion Alcohol, Drug Addiction and Mental Health (ADAMH) Services Board, Judge Robert Fragale with the Marion County Bar Association, and attorney Kevin Hall and Ronald Cramer for helping to fund the Getting Ahead classes at MCI.

Getting Ahead in a Just-Gettin'-By World and *Getting Ahead while Getting Out* wouldn't have been even a dream if it weren't for Ruby Payne, who has been supportive of my efforts from the day we first met in the late 1990s. Many thanks to her and the team at aha! Process: Peggy Conrad, for her calming and reassuring management of this (and other) publications; desktop publisher Paula Nicolella; and editor Dan Shenk of CopyProof. An editor can make or break authors. In this case, we think Dan has been the making of us. For the additional artwork in the workbook we thank our illustrator, Scott Knauer.

Finally, Michelle Wood would like to thank her two boys, Devin and Daylan, for giving her quiet time while she worked on the book. Mitch Libster wishes to thank his wife, Cindy, for her wisdom, patience, and support. And Phil DeVol thanks his wife, Susan, for her feedback, advice, and enduring support.

Philip DeVol, Michelle Wood, and Mitchell Libster

Message from the Authors

What Is *Getting Ahead while Getting Out?*

Getting Ahead while Getting Out is designed to be used by soon-to-be-released offenders, working in groups of 8–12 with one or two trained facilitators, to investigate the impact that poverty and criminal behavior had on them, their families, and the community. *Getting Ahead while Getting Out* is a two-book set: a workbook for returning citizens to use and this *User Guide for Getting Ahead while Getting Out* for sponsors, funders, facilitators, and community collaboratives.

The Origin of *Getting Ahead while Getting Out*

Getting Ahead while Getting Out is based on a workbook that was published in 2004 titled *Getting Ahead in a Just-Gettin'-By World*. That book is in use in communities across the United States and in five other countries. It is being used by social service agencies, faith-based initiatives, courts, employers, healthcare providers, colleges, high schools, early-childhood programs and in correctional facilities.

The Getting Ahead program was so well-received by offenders and correctional officials in facilities in Indiana, Louisiana, Colorado, Ohio, and Maryland that the demand for a book designed specifically for returning citizens began to grow. That demand was first put to Philip DeVol, the author of *Getting Ahead,* by a returning citizen and a Getting Ahead graduate at a National Bridges Out of Poverty Conference in Indianapolis in 2012. She asked if I would consider writing Getting Ahead directed for inmates. Apparently I smiled and said OK but "left it hanging." She went on to explain how recidivism was tied to the lack of resources and the lack of solid reentry plans. From then on, whenever we met, she brought it up until finally I broke down. That woman was Michelle Wood, now the co-author of *Getting Ahead while Getting Out* and the *User Guide*. She joined me and Mitchell Libster, a retired Legal Aid attorney, in writing both books. Mitch and Michelle have co-facilitated Getting Ahead groups in Ohio prisons.

A Pre-Release Book and Long-Term Support for Returning Citizens and Their Families

It's important for readers to know that *Getting Ahead in Just-Gettin'-By World* did not stand alone. It's not enough to engage people in poverty and returning citizens and expect them to change their thinking and be able to overcome the many barriers to stability that they encounter. People in the institutions, such as the those mentioned above, also need to be engaged. They are encouraged to change their mindsets and to work shoulder to shoulder with returning citizens to build communities where everyone can live well. Those communities use the concepts described in the book *Bridges Out of Poverty* to make institutional changes and build Bridges collaboratives. Those collaboratives develop a comprehensive approach to poverty in all its complexities and provide long-term support for Getting Ahead graduates. It occurred to the authors that those Bridges Communities also could be a natural support system for returning citizens.

The Complete Getting Out Reentry Model

With that in mind, we developed the Getting Ahead while Getting Out (hereafter often referred to simply as Getting Out) Reentry Model. The *Getting Ahead while Getting Out* workbook is the key element of the model, but the model goes on to offer Getting Ahead in a Just-Gettin'-By World to the families of the returning citizens so that they have a shared learning experience and language. Returning citizens and their families can utilize the support of Bridges Collaboratives in communities where such initiatives exist. And where they do not exist, planners, such as you, can develop Bridges work. Another option described in the model is for the planners to join or create a reentry program. Our model needs to be flexible, not competitive, and able to utilize the strengths and services of each particular local community.

Research shows that offenders who reach the three-year mark without reoffending are no more likely to break the law than people who have never been in prison. Therefore, the Getting Out Reentry Model is a comprehensive solution that can support returning citizens for three years.

Certified Facilitators for Getting Out, Data Collection, Outcome Reports, and Becoming a Learning Community

A commitment to supporting returnees and reducing recidivism in a comprehensive way requires adherence to the model, high performance standards, and quality improvement practices based on collecting data and reporting on outcomes. Read the section on "Evaluations and Reports" to learn about low-cost data collection options. To learn how to become a certified Getting Out facilitator, see Appendix 8 (Getting Ahead Network website).

How to Get the Most Out of This Book

Ideally everyone—sponsors, funders, community collaboratives, and facilitators—will read the whole book. But to get started, begin by reading the sections that especially relate to your role.

This *User Guide* has three major sections:

The first section describes the philosophy and process of the *Getting Ahead while Getting Out* workbook. It covers how to organize and run the initiative, as well as how to organize a community collaborative based on the Bridges Out of Poverty model (for people in the institution and the community) and Getting Ahead for returning citizens. It's filled with information for sponsors, funders, community collaboratives, and facilitators. Everyone should read this section.

The second part of the book provides special information for facilitators, with module-by-module instructions. This is a must-read for sponsors and facilitators, with sections about how to work with corrections staff that community collaboratives should read.

The third section of the book is the Appendix and Index. Readers will be directed to the Appendix as needed. Look here for the Model Fidelity elements and examples from the providers of web- and cloud-based evaluations and reports. Look into the Index to quickly find information on topics that interest you or are particularly relevant to your involvement in this effort.

Why Would You Take on So Much Work?

People come to this work from many directions. Some come from their own experience in incarceration or the experience of having a family member incarcerated, some from a sense of fairness and justice, some are motivated by their faith, and some want to build better communities. It will take all of us to build successful reentry initiatives.

We acknowledge that this is going to take a lot of work. If you are feeling overwhelmed, please know that you don't need to have every bit of this in place before you begin. Start with finding a few like-minded people and get going with Getting Ahead while Getting Out. Then add the pieces of the model as you go. Also know that you will be supported by the authors of these two books, the consultants at aha! Process, Inc., and the growing learning community that focuses on both poverty and reentry issues.

Thank you for your commitment to helping build communities where everyone can live well.

Philip DeVol, with Michelle Wood and Mitchell Libster

Getting Ahead: What It's About

Overview

People who are returning to the community from incarceration, like others who are living in unstable and stressful situations, are needed at the planning and decision-making tables in our communities. Planners need accurate and relevant information upon which to build programs and base policies, and only those returning to the community have the information about the situations they face each day.

Getting Ahead while Getting Out can help prepare returning citizens to take their seat at planning and decision-making tables and to work shoulder to shoulder to solve community problems.

> *Getting Ahead itself must be relevant, respectful, challenging, safe, and empowering if it is going to engage men and women who will soon be returning their communities.*

Over the years Getting Ahead in a Just-Gettin'-By World, on which Getting Out is based, has proved to be a transformative experience for both participants (known as investigators) and facilitators. At the base of this is the concept of co-investigation—where investigator and facilitator learn together. In Getting Ahead, facilitators do not come at their work as the "sage on the stage" but as the "guide on the side."

When the concept of co-investigation is extended to sponsors, Bridges Collaboratives, and reentry programs, they also will become open to the stories, knowledge, and insights of the investigators. Graduates and facilitators will tell you that co-investigations create a learning experience like few others.

Further, the topics of poverty, prosperity, recidivism, and community sustainability are so compelling that you as a facilitator or sponsor will likely be challenged to expand your exploration of the topics and add to your reading list. This is not a scripted curriculum; it requires additional and deeper learning on your part.

If we agree on the philosophy—the set of underlying concepts and principles—it will allow us to be flexible yet consistent in how we present the information.

Philosophy of Getting Ahead

The outcome we expect from Getting Out is a reduction in recidivism rates, but the underlying goal is to see returning citizens take charge of their own lives.

This is expressed best by Richard Shaull in the foreword to *Pedagogy of the Oppressed* (Freire, 1970):

> There is no such thing as a *neutral* educational process. Education either functions as an instrument that is used to facilitate the integrations of the younger generation into the logic of the present system and bring about conformity to it, *or* it becomes "the practice of freedom," the means by which men and women deal critically and creatively with reality and discover how to participate in the transformation of their world. (p. 16)

One reason typical efforts to reduce poverty and recidivism have not worked is that they fail to talk about and examine the realities of the impact that poverty and instability have on people. Instead, they go straight to teaching the logic of the present system through classes in literacy, financial knowledge, job-seeking skills, workplace skills, and the like. Getting Ahead is unique in that it deals with all the causes of poverty and low resources and trusts the investigators to analyze their situation, to solve problems, and to help transform their communities.

The philosophy that Getting Ahead is built upon has been confirmed and validated by the investigators themselves. Investigators learn by using life itself as the primary context for their learning. They have proven to be problem solvers, not only in their own lives but also in their communities. They have claimed their future stories and are finding their voice and power.

Further, we think the book *Bridges Out of Poverty: Strategies for Professionals and Communities* helps bring about a shift in thinking for those in middle class and wealth. But for them the shift isn't about taking charge of one's own life, it's recognizing the value of the gifts, talents, knowledge, insights, and leadership that returning citizens and people from poverty can offer, and it is making room for them at the decision-making tables.

Philosophies are often very involved and complex. In a way, ours is too, but it helps to state the case in as few words as possible, to boil it down to its essential ideas. Our philosophy starts with the way we understand the situation.

Poverty and unstable situations can trap people in the "tyranny of the moment," making it very difficult to attend to abstract information or plan for the future—the very things needed to stabilize one's environment and build adequate resources and financial assets. There are many causes of poverty, some having to do with the choices of the individual, but many stemming from community conditions, exploitation, and political/economic structures. The philosophy must take all of this into account.

We need an accurate perception of how poverty impacts individuals and communities and an understanding of economic realities as a starting point both for reasoning and for developing plans for transition. Using mental models for comprehension and reasoning, people can move from the concrete to the abstract. Analyzing research on the causes of poverty prepares us to develop comprehensive solutions at the community level. Using Ruby Payne's description of the resources necessary for a full life and her insights into the hidden rules of economic class, people can evaluate themselves, choose behaviors, and make plans to stabilize their environments and build resources for a better life. The community also must provide services, support, and meaningful opportunities over the long term. In partnership with people from middle class and wealth, individuals in poverty can solve community and systemic problems that contribute to poverty.

We will be sharing this philosophy with the participants so they will understand what is being done in Getting Ahead—and so they can monitor their own progress as we move through the workbook.

What follows is an expanded explanation of the philosophy. The writers named in parentheses contributed to our understanding of the principles. Their works can be found in the bibliography of the *Getting Ahead* workbook.

- **Living in chronically unstable conditions or in persistent poverty can make it hard for people to change. Poverty traps people in the tyranny of the moment where concrete problems demand immediate, concrete solutions.** The investigators will complete "Mental Models of Poverty" and "My Life upon Release" that describe concrete living experiences that drive people into the tyranny of the moment and can rob them of their future stories.

  Principle: Instability in daily life focuses attention on concrete issues, all of which doesn't leave much time for abstract pursuits (Payne, Freire, Feuerstein, Galeano).

  Principle: Mental models help people learn quickly and without over-reliance on language (Payne, Freire, Feuerstein, Sapolsky, Mattaini).

- **People in poverty and returning citizens are problem solvers.** People in poverty solve immediate, concrete problems every day using reactive problem-solving skills and relationships.

  Principle: An accurate perception of under-resourced people is that they are problem solvers, as opposed to the prevailing perception that defines them as needy and deficient (McKnight, Pransky, Henderson).

- **Abstract thinking can free investigators from the tyranny of the moment and allow them to separate themselves from their problems, to detach and become objective, to analyze their situations, to learn new information, to make their own arguments for change, and to do proactive planning.**

  Principle: The Getting Ahead Theory of Change (Farson, Freire, Miller & Rollnick, Taylor-Ide & Taylor, DeVol).

- **When offenders and others in unstable environments investigate the multiple causes of poverty, they learn that poverty is caused by more than the choices of the individual.**

  Principle: The research identifies many causes of poverty; therefore, there must be a wide array of strategies to counteract and reduce poverty (O'Connor, Brouwer, Gans).

  Principle: The process of change is enhanced if the person can separate the problem from himself/herself (Freedman & Combs).

- **It's important to learn how poverty and criminal behavior impacts individuals, families, children and the community.** So ... learning about the hidden rules of economic class, resources, and language issues is crucial to doing a critical analysis of the situation.

  Principle: Payne's hidden rules of economic class are a unique, analytical category regarding economic issues. Other categories include race, gender, ethnicity, age, disability, sexual orientation, and immigration status. The hidden rules can be used to navigate new environments, resolve conflicts, and build relationships of mutual respect and social capital (Payne).

- **Doing a "Self-Assessment of Resources" and an "Assessment of Community Resources" will help individuals make plans for economic stability for themselves and their communities.**

  Principle: Ultimately, the work of assessing and planning for all aspects of one's life lies with the individual (Freire, Andreas, Faulkner, Freedman & Combs, Miller & Rollnick).

- **The information in Getting Ahead, the discussions around the table, and the Theory of Change will help investigators break out of the tyranny of the moment and develop a new future story for themselves.**

  Principle: People in unstable situations can be trusted to make good use of accurate information presented in a meaningful way by facilitators who offer a relationship of mutual respect and act as co-investigators (Freire, Sapolsky, McKnight, Pransky, Farson).

  Principle: Individuals must generate their own motivation and plans for change (Miller & Rollnick). Getting Ahead is an agenda-free learning experience where no one will tell an individual what to do.

Principle: Mental models can be used to help people living in poverty move from the concrete to the abstract in order to find new, yet concrete, solutions (Freire, Harrison & Huntington, Payne).

- Using the investigations conducted by the group, individuals will be able to make plans to build resources.

Principle: When investigators use Payne's definitions of hidden rules and resources, they will be able to develop plans to build their own internal and external assets (Payne).

- Partnerships with the middle class and those in wealth will build crucial social capital.

Principle: Bridging social capital is closely linked to success in life. Building a network of diverse people with whom investigators can have relationships of mutual respect is something investigators can do fairly quickly (Fussell, Putnam).

Principle: Individuals who are in the process of developing their own economic security need support to stabilize situations during transitions (Payne).

- The impact of poverty on institutions and communities is similar to its impact on individuals. Developing strategies that also address poverty at the institutional and community levels will give communities a comprehensive approach.

Principle: Institutions and communities that experience instability and have low resources are often pressed into the tyranny of the moment, just as individuals are. The responses of the leaders often are to give up abstract thinking in order to solve immediate, concrete problems by using reactive strategies and to give up the long view in exchange for "short-termism" (DeVol).

Principle: A partnership among all three economic classes is needed to bring about economic stability (Phillips).

Description: The 'Kitchen Table' Learning Experience

Picture a group of people sitting around a table. They may be in a correctional facility, jail, halfway house, treatment-in-lieu-of-incarceration program, outpatient reentry program or a community-based correctional facility (CBCF).

They just finished a meal and are now in a deep conversation. Investigators and facilitators frequently eat together. Sometimes the facilitators bring in food, sometimes they eat food from the kitchen of the correctional facility.

They are leaning forward, listening to first one person talk and then another. On the table are their *Getting Ahead while Getting Out* workbooks, flipchart paper, a dictionary or two, a calculator, and lots of colored markers. On the walls are several mental models drawn on flipchart paper, evidence of the group's work. You might have to watch for a while before you pick out who is facilitating the group. Sometimes one of the facilitators is an offender who has graduated from Getting Ahead (GA). This is the typical "kitchen table" learning experience shared by GA investigators and facilitators.

The group meets two to four times during orientation and 20 times during GA. Then there is a graduation celebration. The group meets once or twice a week for 2½ to 3 hours each time. It's a "closed group," meaning all members start Getting Ahead together, and they stay together until the work is done. It also means that there are no outsiders or observers. To create this scene you need to know these things about Getting Ahead:

> 'The things I have learned in this course are not everyday lessons. They are not common sense. The average person has no idea about the world we live in. Now I am teaching my children so they don't experience what I went through. Once you know, you know, and you can never see the world the same way again.'
>
> —Tanavia Hodges, College Student

Getting Out facilitators are certified. They usually come from outside the institution. Often they are volunteers; sometimes they are working for an organization that is in good standing with the correctional facility.

We've found that it's best to have two facilitators. Often one of them could be a Getting Ahead graduate and returning citizen. The returnee provides credibility with investigators, along with knowledge and insights that are vital for the facilitator who has not experienced incarceration. Both facilitators must be certified in order to offer Getting Ahead.

Conduct Getting Ahead sessions in a safe, agenda-free, and respectful setting. Ideally the room would be "private" in the sense that others would not be looking into the room or coming into the room or passing through it. The room would be big enough to seat everyone comfortably but small enough to provide a sense of intimacy. The room should have wall space to hang flipchart papers that represent that group's evolving work.

Ten years of experience tells us that the group size should be between 8 and 12, but no fewer than 8 and no more than 12. We've learned that about half of the learning in Getting Ahead comes from the content, and half comes from the discussions. Too few people will limit the variety of ideas and input; too many limits the opportunity for everyone to be heard. The closer the group size is to 12 the better.

Jay says it well. The "kitchen table" learning experience can be transformative for everyone involved in the process, which is the focus of the next section.

> 'There are many services that feed people and provide material assistance. But I wanted to be involved in relationships that sustain dignity and mutual support. I wanted to participate in a discovery process that changes lives. The past 15 weeks have not only been fascinating discussions, but we have had fun. I have learned as much in this group as everyone else! We all feel proud of our accomplishments.'
>
> —Jay Wall, GA Facilitator, Billings, MT

Continuum of Those Who Take Part in Getting Ahead

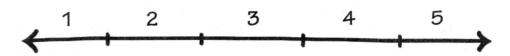

Extremely Unstable Environments

Daily life disrupted by violence, illness, addiction, disabilities, and/or unstable community conditions. Highly affected by generational poverty. Stabilizing the environment and building resources may take a very long time.

Unstable Environments

Daily life can be stabilized enough with supports to attend weekly or bi-weekly workshops. People in generational and situational poverty. Building resources may take a long time.

Fairly Stable Environments

Daily life can be organized fairly easily. May be able to build resources rather quickly. Some people in situational poverty.

Getting Ahead: What It's About

The Process: How It Works

Many of the things that make Getting Ahead work would be invisible to casual observers. After all, they would be seeing people sitting around a table drawing mental models, doing activities in their workbooks, and talking. The following pages explain the rationale behind what occurs in the workbook and everything it takes to set up and run a GA initiative. It's a description of the GA model for those responsible for it—namely, sponsors, facilitators, funders, and community collaboratives, such as Bridges Steering Committees and reentry programs.

Unique features of GA are identified in four charts that appear before we move into the module-by-module instructions. Those charts are:

a. Unique Features of GA Learning Experience
b. Unique Features of Bridges Structures and Operations
c. Unique Features of Community Support Based on Bridges Model
d. Unique Features of GA Content

Facilitators and sponsors may use these charts to plan, monitor, and evaluate their GA initiatives. They can serve as reference points to steady your thinking and focus.

1. Unique Features of GA Learning Experience

UNIQUE FEATURES	BRIEF EXPLANATIONS
Getting Ahead is agenda-free. Investigators make their own arguments for change.	Investigators are not told or forced to change or comply. This approach differs from the "righting reflex" of many middle-class organizations and individuals who try to change or fix things (make them "right") for people in poverty.
Getting Ahead facilitates learning. GA is based on the concept of co-investigation, where investigators and the facilitator learn together.	Facilitators don't do for investigators what they can do for themselves, and they don't decide for investigators what they can decide for themselves.
About half of the learning in Getting Ahead comes from the content and half from the discussions.	The more diversity (age, gender, ethnicity, disability, sexual orientation, situational and generational poverty) at the table, the richer the dialogue. Getting Ahead provides a relevant, respectful, challenging, safe, and empowering experience.
Getting Ahead has two story lines: the personal story and the community story.	Poverty is never just about the individual; it occurs in communities that have varying resources, access, opportunity, support, and leadership.
Getting Ahead addresses relevant economic class issues and uses life itself as the principal context for education.	Getting Ahead deals with the realities of political/economic structures that contribute to and exacerbate poverty. GA trusts the investigators to analyze their situation, to solve problems, and to transform their world.

continued on next page

continued from previous page

1. Unique Features of GA Learning Experience

UNIQUE FEATURES	BRIEF EXPLANATIONS
Getting Ahead uses mental models so investigators can contribute to the body of knowledge and learn quickly, without overreliance on the formal register of language.	Investigators, regardless of their literacy skills, can contribute to the learning experience by participating in discussions and the development of mental models.
Key concepts in Getting Ahead are sequenced and reinforced throughout the 10 modules.	Investigators have several opportunities to deal critically and creatively with the harshest realities of poverty.
The My Life upon Release Mental Model conceptualizes the discrepancy between what life is like now and what life could be.	The discrepancy between what life is like now and what it could be creates the cognitive dissonance that can be the foundational catalyst for change.

The core constructs in more detail

1. *Shared philosophy:* In the GA philosophy at the outset of this section we laid the foundation of constructs and principles for Getting Ahead. It's a shared view of the impact that poverty and incarceration has on individuals and what it takes for someone to make the transition out of poverty and incarceration.

2. *Co-investigation:* To use the philosophy it's crucial that the facilitators see themselves as learners right along with the other group members. Experienced facilitators wholeheartedly agree with this statement. Lowering professional boundaries and being willing to share one's own experiences is necessary. This work is about building bridging social capital, and facilitators often develop that reciprocity with some of the investigators. You might say that when you bring the donuts to the workshop, you are the facilitator; the rest of the time you are a co-investigator!

3. *Safe environment and group rules:* This work is very challenging; there will be difficult conversations. Getting Ahead needs to be a safe place for such hard work. Holding the workshop in a room should provide a sense of intimacy without being overcrowded. Meeting at a lone table in a cavernous room or squeezing together with little personal space is not recommended. Group rules that are set during orientation and confirmed at the first gathering will create a sense of safety. In most groups there are people who have group experience; they will help with the list. The facilitator, as a member of the group, can suggest rules that are important to him/her. One of the first chart papers that is hung on the wall will contain the group rules. It will, like the subsequent mental models, go up every time the group meets.

4. *Half and half:* Facilitators and GA graduates agree that, as a general rule, about half of the learning in Getting Ahead is in the content, and half is in the discussions. Be mindful of the need for this balance.

As facilitators we must begin by listening, by reversing the flow of information. Listening bridges distrust and builds relationships. We don't leap to obvious conclusions or give people "the" solutions. People in poverty get enough of that from the middle class. Action arises out of the meaning of the dialogue.

In the first meeting of the group, the facilitator will want to be listening to the group talk about what poverty is like in the community they will be returning to within minutes of passing out the books.

5. *Sequence and reinforcement:* Getting Ahead is presented in a particular sequence. It follows the pathway laid out by the first few groups to investigate poverty. It is important to follow the sequence and to reinforce the learning as you move along. Jane Vella (2002), author of *Learning to Listen, Learning to Teach,* says,

> When we work diligently to design learning tasks that are in simple and sound sequence and that reinforce learning, we address the disparity in political power more directly than if we preach loudly on social and economic injustice. These rather technical principles and practices—reinforcement and sequence—are tough to use. They demand attention and diligence to design. When you do that hard work, you are in fact addressing sociopolitical-economic inequalities. It is all of a piece. (pp. 13–14)

Five learning sequences get reinforced throughout Getting Ahead. Sequenced learning is the reason Getting Ahead needs to be presented in the order in which it appears and why nothing should be left out. Sponsors and facilitators, driven as they are by costs, have been known to do Getting Ahead in half the time and at half the cost. It's the result of being in middle class, no doubt, so these folks are to be forgiven. However, facilitators and sponsors have reported that Getting Ahead doesn't work very well when you cut parts out.

It's not absolutely necessary that the facilitator knows the five sequences, because they function naturally as the curriculum unfolds. But for those who want to know the sequences, they are presented in Appendix 1. However, it would be a mistake to "reveal" the sequences to the investigators. That would be connecting the dots for the investigators, robbing them of the pleasure of making their own discoveries.

6. *The Process Triangle:* The mental model of the learning process appears in the Introduction of the *GA* workbook. It describes how this process is presented. In a nutshell it works like this:
   - Learn about poverty and incarceration in the broad sense
   - Learn about the hidden rules of class
   - Learn about language and resources
   - Learn how poverty and incarceration impacts you
   - Assess your own resource
   - Assess your own risk factors
   - Assess community resources
   - Think about it; analyze it
   - Make your plans for building resources
   - Monitor your motivation and your changes throughout

The Triangle is used at the beginning of each module to help the investigators connect the topic to the larger learning experience.

7. *The purpose of each module:* The modules advance the work in two ways: through the content and through the process. This is described in a paper titled "Getting Ahead—the Purpose of Each Module," which is available in Appendix 2. Facilitators can use this paper to evaluate and monitor the progress of their group.

8. *Two storylines:* Facilitators will be working with two storylines throughout the GA workbook. One is the collective story of all incarcerated people and those in poverty and the local community. The second storyline applies to individuals: their history, the impact that poverty and incarceration has had on them, and the degree to which they do without specific resources.

The community story is invariably easier to talk about than the personal or individual story so in Getting Ahead the community issues are typically addressed first. For example, the first mental model in Module 1 is about poverty and incarceration. Only after doing a number of activities do the investigators do a mental model of their own lives.

9. *Separate the problem from the person:* In Getting Ahead the strategy is to be objective about the problems we face. It's easier to make changes if you aren't seen as the problem. A key role of the facilitator is to separate the problem from the person.

In *Narrative Therapy: The Social Construction of Preferred Realities* (1996), Jill Freedman and Gene Combs suggest that the way questions are asked can facilitate change. When we ask, "How has poverty and/or incarceration affected you?" we help create intellectual distance or detachment that *facilitates change.* This is different from laying the blame for a person's circumstances on him/her directly, as if poverty had everything to do with the choices of the poor and nothing to do with larger community and national factors. Framing the questions in this way means that group members don't have to defend themselves.

10. *Group process:* Groups tend to act in predictable ways. The phases of most groups include:

    a. *Forming*—Everyone tries to earn the respect of the leader and be helpful.

    b. *Storming*—The rules are tested and people assert their independence.

    c. *Norming*—Patterns, rules, and unspoken rules are established and adhered to.

    d. *Performing*—The members work hard, building on each other's ideas; people begin to appreciate each other.

> 'People in poverty might need to change—but no more than anyone else in our society.'
> —Philip DeVol

Experienced facilitators will tell you that every GA group is different. While you can trust that good things will come of Getting Ahead, you can't assume that every group will respond to the content of each module in the same way.

The same is true for the group process. You can count on it, but it will unfold differently. Facilitators say that most groups are *performing* during or by the end of Module 3, which could be the sixth time the group meets.

11. *Concrete to abstract to concrete:* People in unstable environments live in a concrete environment. But if they're going to make changes, they need to be in the abstract where they can get new ideas. So we offer the abstract in the form of (a) research on the causes of poverty, (b) Ruby Payne's information about resources and hidden rules, and (c) information on how change takes place.

    For people caught up in (or bogged down by) the tyranny of the moment, it's difficult to find the time to devote to abstract pursuits. An examination of mental models of class (i.e., the environments of class) will show that people in middle class usually have enough time (and money) to be involved in politics, hobbies, and the educational activities of their children. In wealth, time can be given to the arts, travel, social clubs, and events, in addition to politics, hobbies, and education. In Module 3 facilitators will draw the Theory of Change Mental Model and explain how investigators can choose to give time to the abstract even when they're in survival mode.

    In Getting Ahead the starting point in every module is to establish the relevance of the material. The activities move back and forth between the concrete and the abstract using mental models, assessments, worksheets, stories, and dialogue.

12. *Mental models and literacy:* Mental models are stories, parables, analogies, metaphors, cartoons, charts, physical movements, and drawings. We use mental models from beginning to end in Getting Ahead. In fact, the very first group activity (after introductions and developing group rules) is to create a Mental Model of Poverty. The last thing we do as a group is build a Mental Model of Community Prosperity.

    We use mental models because:

    a. They move us from the concrete to the abstract. The Mental Model of Poverty contains concrete information about poverty. As group members "step back" from the drawing and begin to analyze it, they have moved to the abstract.

b. They free us from a reliance on the written word and formal register. This means that Getting Ahead will also work for investigators who don't read well. Group members will often take turns reading passages from the workbook. Those who cannot read well are welcome to pass. During activities that do require reading, the facilitator may need to read the questions to the individuals who cannot read well, while the rest of the group works individually. This is when having a co-facilitator would be especially helpful.

c. They simplify the information, and yet they contain a great deal of information. The mental models are taped to the wall every session so they can be used to reinforce learning. New information can be added to them as the group deepens its understanding of the issues.

d. They shift the work of learning to the group. One of the unique features of Getting Ahead is that facilitators never do for adult learners what they can do for themselves. The group takes ownership of the information that goes into the mental models. And the mental models document the group's work.

e. They are easy to carry in the mind, to remember. They are much easier to remember than blocks of text.

f. They speed learning. Building a mental model takes more time than lecturing or reading, so it seems counterintuitive that they would speed learning. But taking the time to create a mental model means not having to keep repeating the information or rereading the material.

g. Finally, mental models free us from lectures and the *yak, yak, yak* of the middle class. And mental models are great tools for facilitators who don't want to fall into the role of teacher.

By the way, don't think of mental models as a "remedial" teaching tool. They have been adopted by the business world through the work of respected writers and consultants like David Baum, Margaret Wheatley, Joseph Jaworski, and Peter Senge.

Mental models are a map of how we see the world. Peter Senge (1990) describes mental models as theories-in-use. Some are simple generalizations, and some are complicated, but they determine how we act: "The problems with mental models lie not in whether they are right or wrong—by definition, all models are simplifications. The problems with mental models arise when the models are tacit—when they exist below the level of awareness" (p. 176). If you aren't aware of your mental models, you can't challenge them, and so they become a barrier to learning. They keep you frozen where you are.

The mental models generated by GA groups are used to challenge the thinking of people who aren't aware of their own inaccurate understanding of poverty. This is of huge significance; the mental models created by GA investigators have already changed the thinking of thousands of people who attend Bridges workshops. The facilitators use a Mental Model of Poverty that is a compilation of many mental models created by GA investigators. The mental models created by each GA group can be used to change the thinking of people in their own communities.

In GA groups we will create a series of personal and group mental models as the investigations unfold. The facilitator must make sure the group models are stored and put on the walls at each session so investigators can build on them, revise them, and discover connections between and among them.

> *'An insight is a restructuring of information; it's seeing the same old thing in a completely new way.*
>
> *'Once that restructuring occurs, you never go back.'*
>
> —Earl Miller,
> Massachusetts Institute
> of Technology

13. ***Language:*** In Getting Ahead we explore information that is valuable for people of all classes. The information applies directly and is relevant to investigators. Many GA graduates have said that they were able to immediately use the information on language at school, work, and with their children.

    We cover information on registers of language, discourse patterns, story structures, code switching, voices, early-childhood language experience, and negotiation skills. We hope to give investigators a way to analyze and act on their strengths and weaknesses.

    Language can separate us by class, or it can be used to bring us together. We trust that the information on language will help prepare investigators to analyze new environments, negotiate them skillfully, and build relationships of mutual respect with people from diverse backgrounds. When they join other problem solvers at the decision-making tables in our communities, we want the investigators to be prepared.

    Building a vocabulary is just one way to do that. In each module of Getting Ahead, we provide a list of potentially new words found in the module. New words will be defined when they're first used. The facilitator can assist investigators to be more word-conscious by having investigators underline words that are new to them, modeling an interest in new words, using correct pronunciation, and playing with words.

14. ***Critical analysis—moving from situated cognition to a culture of learning:*** Earlier we defined education as "…the means by which men and women deal critically and creatively with reality and discover how to participate in the transformation of their world." The following chart, adapted from the *Investigations into Economic Class in America* workbook, illustrates the process that many investigators go through as they become confident learners.

    The workbook begins by "meeting the students where they are" and honoring the knowledge about poverty they bring to the classroom.

    The process creates learner-generated content "not prescribed by teachers acting as dispensers of information but rather content discovered and created by the students as they become actively engaged in the construction of the knowledge base they perceive to be needed in their real world" (pp. 7–8). Krodel et al. go on to say:

    > This participation creates a shared repertoire of vocabulary, communal routines, and behaviors (Wenger, 1999) and fosters the relationships and extra support needed to move to formalized or decontextualized education (p. 7). … Indeed, this approach to learning prepares students for their new roles in school and society by using life itself as the context for education rather than positioning education as the preparation necessary for life. (p. 8)

    The chart on the following page outlines how the major elements of Getting Ahead interact to effect this change.

Changing Thinking from Situated Cognition to a Culture of Learning

	Beginning stages of Getting Ahead 'Just plain folks'	Intermediate and ending phase of Getting Ahead Student	Ending phase and post-Getting Ahead Practitioner
Reasons with	**Casual stories** Investigators examine personal stories as the context for the course	**Laws** Investigators apply hidden rules of economic class to understand their past and present societal experience	**Causal models** Investigators use the poverty Research Continuum and process of change as analytical frameworks to support abstract arguments
Acting on	**Situations** Investigators act on current situations, building bonding relationships and peer support within the group	**Symbols** Investigators create mental models reflecting personal and community resources, building bridging relationships; investigators increase their support for each other	**Conceptual situations** Increasingly complicated mental models represent social, political, and economic issues to address
Resolving	**Emergent problems and dilemmas** Investigators apply new learning and accept support from new relationships	**Well-defined problems** Investigators proactively plan and collaborate to meet goals and build resources identified in personal resource assessment	**Ill-defined problems** Investigators engage in and seek new relationships to support plans and solve problems identified in personal and community resource assessment; they predict problems and are proactive in approaching new situations
Producing	**Negotiable meaning and socially constructed understanding** Investigators build community and shared language to understand economic class	**Fixed meaning and immutable concepts** Investigators establish a lexicon and framework of ideas that can be applied to individual plans	**Negotiable meaning and socially constructed understanding** Investigators use new language to reflect on issues, assign meaning, and build new relationships to support change

Source: Adapted from J. S. Brown, A. Collins, and P. Duguid, "Situated Cognition and the Culture of Learning," *Educational Researcher,* 1989, p. 35.

15. *Motivation:* Getting Ahead is for people who are not motivated, as well as those who are. GA sponsors often think that they need to recruit people who are really motivated to make changes in their lives. In this way they expect to use their time and money wisely. Why work with people who are not motivated? This makes sense, of course; but they should know that it's in the Getting Ahead setting that many people "find" their motivation.

Our goal is for the investigators, not us, to make the argument for change. Our process is designed to foster motivation by creating a discrepancy between life as it is now and what it might be in the future. The My Life upon Release Mental Model created in Module 1 is the baseline for that discrepancy-making process. It names, describes, and analyzes the impact of poverty and incarceration on the investigator. Again, we must not allow ourselves to make the argument for change. Resist the urge! The role of the facilitator is described best by William Miller and Stephen Rollnick (2002) in *Motivational Interviewing: Preparing People for Change.*

Carl Rogers articulated and tested a theory about critical counselor skills for facilitating change. He asserted that a client-centered interpersonal relationship—in which the counselor manifests three critical conditions—provides the ideal atmosphere for change to occur. Within the context of such a safe and supportive atmosphere, clients are free to explore their experiences openly and to reach resolutions of their own problems. The counselor's role, in Rogers' view, is not a directive one of providing solutions, suggestions, or analysis. Instead, the counselor need only offer these three critical conditions to prepare the way for natural change: accurate empathy, non-possessive warmth, and genuineness. (p. 6)

The problems the investigators face while incarcerated and upon release usually require immediate action and, when a person must act, he/she may not be willing or able to learn. The security of a middle-class income allows people to know that today's needs are met. Since middle-class people are not living in the tyranny of the moment, they have the luxury of being able to afford to focus on the future and the abstract. People who live in the concrete can motivate themselves to move toward something or away from something. In either case, though, it's an immediate reaction.

So asking people who are incarcerated or from poverty to participate in a program that has some possible distant reward isn't going to work anymore than the "thou shalts" of the middle class have worked. This workbook is about change, and change can be especially difficult for people in poverty. Richard Farson, author of *Management of the Absurd* (1997), says that individuals with the most resources find it easiest to change, while those with the fewest find it hardest. Incidentally, this is true of organizations too. Paradoxically, for people to change (get sober, climb out of poverty, build assets) they have to move from the concrete to the abstract. So ... helping people move into the abstract becomes a key issue. This is addressed in Module 3 where we lay out our Theory of Change.

In Getting Ahead there's a built-in sequence to assist people to find their motivation. It's described in the paper titled "Sequence and Reinforcement of Key Concepts Found in Getting Ahead" in Appendix 1.

16. *Facilitator role as someone from the dominant culture:* Those who have worked on poverty or diversity issues are familiar with the quandary of the facilitator's hierarchical position. There is no escaping two conflicting and co-existing realities. One is the distrust that most people in poverty have for authority and agencies. This can be ameliorated if the facilitator is from poverty, but *only somewhat.* Why? Because the facilitator is an agency employee or a member of some other group and this eliminates automatic credibility. The second reality is that people with more resources and a broader perspective have something of value to offer those who are trapped in the moment. Freire's *Pedagogy of the Oppressed* (1970) contains the deepest exploration of this dilemma and the best guide for an educator or instructor. Dean Lobovits and John Prowell, writing about narrative approaches, offer three points of guidance to the facilitator in their article "Unexpected Journey: Invitations to Diversity."

a. **Defining a dominated group:** Members of a dominated group either share a common fate or are perceived by the dominant group to share a common fate. People from a distinct racial, ethnic, or religious group (such as recent immigrants from Cambodia or Africa) are likely to identify themselves with other immigrants from their country and recognize that their fates are linked. On the other hand, some people in poverty, even those of the same race or ethnic background, may not feel that their fates are linked. In other words, the individual *does* feel part of the dominant culture. Yet, it is the dominant culture that perceives him/her as a member of a group with a shared fate—as with whites in poverty, for example.

The implication for facilitators is this: If we don't acknowledge that some people feel dominated or threatened by us, and if we don't have a way of dealing with the dominator/dominated issue, we will fail to establish the relationships of mutual respect.

In addition, we as facilitators must be aware that, if we aren't careful, we may contribute to the "false generosity" of the dominant culture. False generosity is kindness in return for something. A man who took meals to men living under a bridge was asked, "What do you want? Are you checking up on us?"

False generosity includes the paternalistic attitudes and "caring for" strategies that are frequently used by missionaries to foreign lands. But they're just as real in the mindsets of many people who work with those in poverty in the United States. Earning "jewels in the crown" is the "something" that some people want in return for their generosity.

False generosity also includes seeing the person in poverty as "other" than oneself and thereby retaining one's distance from and rank over them. This often results in treating GA graduates as "stars"—and at the same time never letting them forget that they were once a "client" or "student."

Individuals with false generosity don't like to be disobeyed, criticized, or even questioned by those they help.

True generosity is kindness in return for nothing. Having authentic relationships as co-investigators and fellow problem solvers comes from seeing our fates as linked, even when we come from different socioeconomic environments and backgrounds. Lila Watson, an aboriginal woman from Australia, said, "If you have come to help me, you can go home. But if you see my struggles as a part of your own survival, then perhaps we can work together." This is another reason Getting Ahead is operating at its best when it's agenda-free. If we're frustrated or even angry at GA participants because they didn't "perform" well, it's due to the agenda we put on them—and because our "helpfulness" is the principal "something" we want in return for our generosity.

b. **The fate of the middle class:** The middle class is declining for the first time since the beginning of the Industrial Revolution. Many well-paying manufacturing jobs have gone overseas, and now white-collar, knowledge-sector jobs are going there too. Since 2008 the security and stability of millions of middle-class families have been shaken. Large numbers have lost their housing and doubled up with relatives, and many children who were once middle class are now eligible for free and reduced lunches at school. Several writers on economic issues suggest that the middle class needs to wake up; its fate is now linked to that of the poor.

c. **Raising the difficult issues:** As representatives (in most cases) of the dominant culture, facilitators need to be the ones to raise the issues that usually fall to the people in the dominated group: racism, predatory practices, and discrimination. When those who are dominated are expected to raise these issues, it forces them into the role of complainer or radical—and may even suggest that they are speaking *for* the dominated group. Being forced into those roles takes away from other roles they might play: mediator, creative thinker, or leader. When the facilitator raises a controversial issue, the people from the dominated group are free to respond in any number of ways. In this workbook, the *facilitator* is the one who shares the details and historical trends of inadequate housing, low-wage jobs, and predators. The partnership between a facilitator and co-facilitator, who often acts as a "bridging" person, can serve as an avenue for exploring the information and evaluating the relationship between the facilitator and the group.

Finally it should be noted that, when going through the *GA* workbook, some investigators may for the first time begin to realize they are near poverty—or even in it—and start seeing themselves as part of a group with a shared fate. We have been using the phrases "people living in near poverty" and "people living in unstable environments" synonymously. As facilitators, we need to be aware that this dynamic is occurring because it can be a very meaningful realization for the investigator.

17. *Role of co-facilitator:* The first time you use the workbook, you will be the only facilitator. The second and all subsequent times, you may have one or two co-facilitators from a previous GA group. It's part of our philosophy to utilize GA graduates as co-facilitators, and eventually as "the" facilitator, because they:

    a. Can make the material more relevant
    b. Can help bridge the initial distrust of the group members
    c. Will learn the material more thoroughly by assisting as a co-facilitator
    d. Will be building bridging social capital with you
    e. Can earn the respect of their peers by assisting you
    f. Can help monitor and improve the facilitator's performance

The co-facilitator's role is to:

   a. Participate in the group, just as anyone else does—working on the mental models, doing the exercises, etc.
   b. Model how to explore ideas, how to be a healthy group member
   c. Assist in guiding the activities and discussions
   d. Assist in evaluating and planning each session
   e. Get together with investigators who miss a session to bring them up to speed so that everyone arrives next time ready to go—at the same place in the workbook

18. *The role of the investigators:* Facilitators who used the workbook *Getting Ahead in a Just-Gettin'-By World* in correctional facilities report that investigators begin to bond into a "group" just as they do in community settings. We learned that inmates had many reasons to succeed, and one of them was to make the program, not just themselves, a success.

19. *Trust the process:* The first time you take a group through the workbook you will likely wonder if it's working. Questioning the process and feeling the urge to fix what you might see as broken are natural. However, resist the urge to react to all the things that worry you. After you've gone through the workbook a couple of times, you'll increasingly trust the process and find that many things sort themselves out.

> *'You have to be able to trust. You have to be able to trust yourself. You have to be able to trust the participants. You have to be able to trust the process. And most importantly, trust the curriculum because it's there. Even when you don't see it there, when the participants don't see it there, one piece leads to the next piece. If you fall back on that, if you just let yourself fall into what the curriculum offers, you really will have a journey as a facilitator, and you will be able to experience tremendous growth with your participants.'*
>
> —Mickie Lewis, GA Facilitator, Northeast Colorado

How to Provide Getting Ahead while Getting Out Inside Correctional Facilities

Getting Ahead takes a lot of work. Happily, those who have used Getting Ahead in correctional institutions say it's worth the effort because GA investigators generate energy during the sessions and afterward. They pump more excitement into the reentry efforts than it takes to run the GA workshop.

We mentioned earlier that there is a complete Getting Out Reentry Model. It will be described in the next section. Right now we want to explain the cornerstone of the model, which is the GA workbook. It is the cornerstone because it is used to engage returning citizens in solving the problems of incarceration, recidivism, and poverty.

In communities where there is no collaborative based on Bridges Out of Poverty concepts, the work falls to the sponsoring organization to act as the catalyst. Of course, most GA initiatives in correctional facilities started with one person, one organization, and one Getting Ahead group. The information in this section can serve as a future story for those who are just now getting started.

In communities where there is a Bridges Collaborative and/or a reentry coalition, the work can be shared among the following members: facilitators, sponsors, funders, investigators, and members of the coalition or collaborative. The initiative is stronger when there is a broader sense of ownership.

The team (sponsors, investigators, et al.) must be accountable to the entire group and to each other. Mutual accountability is a key feature of Getting Ahead. Investigators become accountable to each other for doing their share of the investigations, for contributing to the discussions, and for developing information that gets passed on to the community. They are even accountable to the group, not the facilitator, for being on time.

Choice, Power, and Acccountability

The main theme of our work is for investigators to analyze their own situations, assess their own resources, and *choose* their own plans of action. Facilitators will share the hidden rules of class and assist investigators in acquiring the power they need to meet their goals.

Power can take any number of forms, starting with power over oneself, including over one's own thinking and emotions. Then there's the power of language and negotiation and, finally, the power of connections and political/economic influence. Linked to power and choice is responsibility—the responsibility for the outcomes and the actions that are taken. People who live reactive lives and have little opportunity to make significant choices, people who have little power or influence, people who didn't participate in planning or decision making, are not likely to feel responsible for whatever occurs, for the outcomes. On the other hand, people who have practiced making choices and using power throughout their lives are more likely to be accountable to themselves and others.

The third piece, *"accountability,"* is sweeping the land: Fourth-graders and their teachers are held accountable, people who seek work and their caseworkers are held accountable, addicts and their counselors are held accountable. Accountability in its politicized form is greatly debated, often clumsily done, and unevenly administered. For people in poverty, accountability tends to be just another name for punishment; it's simply one more time the middle class "lays down the law." And yet, accountability is a positive attribute when it arises from within the person as a result of his/her use of choice and power. Facilitators need to hold to this form of accountability; it is a far better model than the "caring for" model, which fosters both manipulation and dependency.

Our form of accountability has these characteristics:

- All information is presented in a way that is relevant, including information about accountability. For people in poverty, it has to apply to the concrete situation. This is one reason we hire co-facilitators from earlier classes; they know how to make information more relevant.

- Expectations must be communicated clearly, concretely, and respectfully.

- Ideally, people will be accountable to themselves and others—and especially to the GA group itself.

- The expectations are related to the systems and structures of the group, agency, community, or nation.

- People are met where they are. For example, for those who have mental health difficulties, addiction problems, or some sort of disability, the units of accountability are smaller and more immediate.

- Accountability is framed as choices with natural and logical consequences.

- Support must be provided for people who are learning to be accountable.

- When the above conditions are in place, people are held accountable for their choices. One consequence may be that some can't continue with the workgroup.

When any consequences are applied, they are handled face to face, not by letter. In this way mediation can occur, and there's a better chance the relationship can be maintained.

The following chart provides a bird's-eye view of what is involved in running Getting Ahead. This chart alerts the organizers to the scale of the work and names those responsible for each task. One of the unique features of Getting Ahead is that people from all classes and sectors are engaged in the initiative. It's assumed that GA grads are on the boards and committees that manage the work. Planners should be guided by the phrase, "What's about us, without us, is not for us."

Two Accountability Charts

There is a lot to providing a pre-release learning group and a broader community support system for returning citizens. The two following charts are designed to identify at a glance the roles and responsibilities of the providers.

The two charts are Accountability for Getting Ahead Classes and Accountability for Getting Out Initiative.

Following each chart, detailed information is provided for each of the topics listed in the left-hand column.

Accountability for Getting Ahead Classes					
	Investigators	Facilitators	Sponsors	Funders	Institutions
Budget			X	X	X
Recruiting		X	X		X
Orientation		X	X		X
Meeting Space		X	X		X
Scheduling		X	X		X
Supplies			X		X
Food		X	X		X
Facilitator Support			X		X
Troubleshooting		X	X		X
Poverty and Reentry Information	X	X	X	X	X
Fundraising and Grant Writing			X	X	X
History and Media	X	X	X	X	X
Model Fidelity		X	X	X	X

Budget

It's a common tendency for middle-class organizers to think, *Getting Ahead takes 20 sessions: If I do it in 10 sessions, I can save time and money.* Resist the urge! Others have tried this, and it hasn't worked. Getting Ahead is based on having a safe place to fully discuss the carefully sequenced information; again, half the learning is in the discussion.

Budget line items include fixed costs:

- *Getting Ahead while Getting Out* workbooks for every investigator; for current pricing go to *http://www.ahaprocess.com/store/*
- *User Guide for Getting Ahead while Getting Out* for each facilitator, co-facilitator, and sponsor; for current pricing go to *http://www.ahaprocess.com/store/*

Recruiting

The correctional facility and the providers of Getting Out must collaborate through the entire process—from recruiting to graduation.

When recruiting, we are looking for investigators:

- Who want to attend; do *not* coerce or require participation
- Who will be available from three weeks prior to the first session through the entire 20 sessions. The three weeks prior are needed to interview and select investigators and to provide orientation
- Who have been brought to a new facility and have had at least two weeks to adjust to the institution
- Who will not be released prior to completion; understand that institutions do not always have control over this
- From different races and ethnicities; maintain a balance, if possible, although this varies by institution
- Who have been informed about the philosophy of GA
- Who will be returning to communities where there is an existing Bridges Collaborative or participating reentry program (when and where possible)

When recruiting, the facilitators and corrections staff will:

- Put selection criteria in writing
- Have assigned personnel to work together on the initiative
- Collaborate during selection process
- Adhere to all policies of the facility

Orientation

Orientation will be done with the whole group of selected investigators in one or two three-hour sessions.

Incarcerated individuals learn not to trust others and certainly not to open up their personal lives to others. This can be seen as a sign of weakness, which can be dangerous for them. We cannot expect investigators to open up completely, but a little openness is needed and can be fostered during the GA sessions.

Orientation will be utilized to:

- Inform the investigators about the program
- Introduce the facilitators and explain their reasons for offering GA
- Begin to establish trust between the facilitator and the investigators—and between the investigators
- Explain that half of the learning is in the content and half is in the group conversations
- Explain the GA process using the "Triangle"
- Establish group rules to be used throughout GA
- Establish the philosophy and unique features of Getting Ahead, including:
  - No one will tell them what to do; there is no GA "agenda"

- No one will do for them what they can do for themselves
- No one will make the argument for change for them
- They will assess their own situations
- They will make their own plans for the future
- They are viewed as problem solvers who are needed at the planning tables in their communities
- Post-release supports will be provided according to the community they live in

• Establish the expectations of a GA investigator, including:
  - Attend all sessions
  - Do make-up work if a session is missed; it's important that everyone is at the same place in the process at the same time
  - Be accountable to the group for being on time and completing the work he/she has committed to doing

Finally, investigators can opt out of GA if they decide it isn't for them.

Facilitators who have done GA in correctional facilities report that GA graduates often help recruit for the next session.

Meeting Space

An ideal room would be big enough for a table or tables around which 14 people could sit comfortably. There would be enough wall space to hang flipchart papers that are produced by the group. The room should offer privacy so that people passing by could not see in. Big rooms like dining halls or gymnasiums don't provide a sense of togetherness.

Scheduling

Experience tells us that groups should meet no less than once a week and no more than twice a week. This is largely a cognitive approach, and yet the topics and discussions do bring up feelings. Having time between sessions to work through emotions is necessary.

Supplies

Recommended supplies for the investigators include the *Getting Ahead while Getting Out* workbook, paper, pen, pencil, calculator, dictionary, and calendar. These (even dictionaries) are often available for purchase by facilitators at a discount store. Recommended group supplies include flipchart paper, many colored markers, and masking tape.

Note that all supplies, food, drinks, etc., provided to the investigators are subject to the rules of the institution.

Food

Some food, even if it's only drinks and snacks, is highly recommended. After all, it's a "kitchen table" learning experience.

Facilitator Support

It's helpful to have several people trained as facilitators. Getting Ahead is relationship-based. This means the facilitator—or both facilitators, should they be working as a team—must attend every session. This work is based on relationships, so both facilitators must be there (outside of illness or a family emergency) to hear every conversation and witness the changes in thinking as they occur.

Support for facilitators can include:

- Having a co-facilitator so the two can give each other feedback
- Having meetings of facilitators to form a learning community so best practices can be shared
- Connecting them to the national community of practice of facilitators through the Getting Ahead website and encouraging them to attend the national conference in the fall

Troubleshooting (During the 20 Sessions of Getting Ahead)

Create a written policy for handling problems. **One motto of Getting Ahead sponsors and facilitators could be "Catch problems early."** The link between the facilitators and sponsors should be strong so that problems can be addressed quickly. Part of the problem-solving process can include getting help from the three authors of *Getting Ahead while Getting Out*.

Poverty and Reentry Information

While incarcerated and after returning to the community, Getting Out investigators generate information about conditions and barriers they face. That information is needed by planners and decision makers in the community.

Organizers and sponsors of Bridges and Getting Ahead Collaboratives need to develop a standard practice for including GA graduates in their deliberations. Not just as people who identify problems but as people who can help create solutions.

If returning citizens are not intentionally and formally included, the organizers will tend to revert to the default mode of excluding people who don't work in the institutions.

Fundraising and Grant Writing

When seeking funds organizers will benefit from:

- The evaluation tools described previously that provide local and national data
- The comprehensive Getting Out Reentry Model
- The Getting Ahead Learning Community

Organizers are urged to collaborate with others who are interested in or doing reentry work rather than compete with them for funding. This applies to those doing the same work at the county level, as well as the state level.

Several Getting Ahead while Getting Out sites within a state that share information, results, and innovations will be able to have more influence and attract more funding than those that stand alone.

History and Media

Having a "historian" record events, decisions, key steps, results and celebrations will help inform the community, write grants, and have an impact at the policy level.

Maintaining such a record also will be helpful to communities that are starting a Getting Out initiative, as well as with the media.

Coordinate all media events with the leaders of the correctional facility. Graduation celebrations often appear in local news stories. As Bridges concepts are applied in more sectors (corrections, business, hospital, courts, health, and schools) there will be even more to report. Building relationships with journalists in media outlets can help change mindsets and open additional doors for GA graduates.

Graduates usually have wonderful, creative ways of expressing themselves; they are a powerful resource for educating the public. Experienced sponsors suggest that the publicity work and training work done by GA graduates be shared among those who are interested and capable. Utilizing the same few investigators can turn some people into "stars," thereby unwittingly overlooking others with talent and a desire to help.

Model Fidelity

The sponsor, institution, and facilitator need to check all decisions against the Model Fidelity checklist in the section on the Getting Out Reentry Model. This model will be used in many correctional institutions in many states—and possibly other countries. Consistency is important. If the model isn't used as designed, not only would investigators get short-changed, the reputation of the program could be damaged.

Accountability for Getting Out Initiative					
	Investigators	Facilitators	Sponsors	Funders	Institutions
Getting Out Reentry Model	X	X	X	X	X
Data, Evaluations, Reports, Social Media	X	X	X	X	X

Getting Out Reentry Model

NOTE: This overview is available at *www.ahaprocess.com* as a free download. It can be used to explain and market the model to corrections officials, funders, and the community.

The Vision

To provide citizens returning from incarceration and their families a comprehensive, community- and relationship-based approach to reentry that begins in pre-release and follows through with long-term support.

The goal is to engage previously incarcerated persons, their families, volunteers, community organizations, and people in corrections as problem solvers who work shoulder to shoulder to create communities where everyone can live well.

Where We Started

There are many communities across the United States and in six other countries that use the underlying constructs of this model to help stabilize the lives of those in poverty and near poverty. These collaboarative efforts are called Bridges Communities. They are based on the concepts found in the books *Bridges Out of Poverty* and *Getting Ahead in a Just-Gettin'-By World*—and they're based on the solutions created by those who embedded the concepts in their organizations and communities. Former offenders in these communities already benefit from attending Getting Ahead (also known as GA) workgroups and from the support they receive from Bridges Collaboratives.

Bridges Communities provide comprehensive, "above-the-silos" support that engages sectors of the community that include employers, courts, early-childhood centers, schools, postsecondary institutions, healthcare and mental health facilities, substance abuse programs, social services, and others. Many of these collaboratives are ready and willing to expand their work to support returning citizens. These opportunities led to the determination to offer a complete reentry model for returning citizens and not just a pre-release workbook.

Getting Ahead in a Just-Gettin'-By World, on which *Getting Ahead while Getting Out* is based, was first published in 2004, with revisions in 2006 and 2013. The Getting Ahead approach has been used successfully in correctional facilities in Indiana, Louisiana, Colorado, Ohio, and Maryland, encouraging the production of a workbook specific to the problems and challenges of reentry.

The Getting Out Model offers a common language for analyzing and acting on economic and community realities.

The Getting Out Reentry Model Is Grounded in Five Principles

Principle #1

Everyone is seen as a *problem solver and co-creator,* including returning citizens, their families, professionals from corrections, reentry program staff and volunteers, and members of Bridges Collaboratives. Relationship-based approaches that build social capital across racial and class lines is foundational to a successful community approach.

Example: Everyone involved has access to the planning and decision-making tables to share information, identify problems, and create solutions.

Decision-making responsibilities remain at the individual, agency, and community levels. Under the collaborative approach, however, input is received and others' interests are taken into account. Having direct input from those who are reentering the community is vital.

Principle #2

The *shared language of Bridges and Getting Ahead,* made up of core constructs and commonly held mental models for complex issues, enhances the effectiveness and sustainability of the initiative.

Example: Individuals, institutions, and communities can use Bridges concepts to analyze problems and develop solutions, programs, and policies that provide a foundation that is consistent across sectors.

A common language used by the community makes it possible to establish long-term (25-year) commitments. Community and organizational initiatives become deeply rooted and don't have to live and die with the leaders who come and go. Everyone owns the Bridges Constructs, and nobody owns the Bridges Constructs. It is a shared movement.

Principle #3

A *comprehensive approach,* starting with a pre-release program through stabilization upon release and the development of resources over time, is essential.

Example: All causes of recidivism and poverty must be addressed, including (1) individual choices and circumstances, (2) community and neighborhood conditions, (3) predatory practices, and (4) political/economic structures.

This approach attracts both people who are conservative and those who are progressive/liberal, because it isn't an either/or approach to the causes of recidivism and poverty. This model is "both/and," thereby honoring the good research on the causes of poverty from the continuum that runs from individual choice and responsibility at one end to systemic factors at the other.

Principle #4

A comprehensive reentry model must be *flexible* to account for existing programs, local conditions, history, leadership, and resources.

Example: An effective model needs to engage existing programs rather than compete with them—utilizing and collaborating with providers who adhere to best-practices methodology.

Communities can build the Getting Out Model over time, adding elements until the complete model is in place. They also can act more quickly by partnering with existing programs, enhancing reentry by combining necessary elements.

Principle #5

The Getting Out Model must be *data-driven.* Two national web-based providers serving Bridges Communities are available for those using the Getting Out Model.

Example: Evidence of effectiveness includes a hope scale, stability scale, and a resources development scale for 11 quality-of-life indicators. In addition, the evaluation tools report on ROI (return on investment) data and a model fidelity scale.

Local and national data are available to the Getting Out sites. The data can be used to support a national learning community of all the Getting Out sites that also share best practices. On the next page we list a number of resources that comprise elements of the **Getting Out Model.**

- A two-book set for offenders and those who provide the Getting Out program is available. *Getting Ahead while Getting Out* is a workbook for soon-to-be-released returnees in which they will develop a 72-Hour Stability Plan and SMART Plan to build 11 resources over time. This accompanying *User Guide for Getting Ahead while Getting Out* is for those who organize, sponsor, fund, and facilitate the workbook. Trainer certification for facilitators of Getting Out will be provided.

- A similar two-book set, *Getting Ahead in a Just-Gettin'-By World* and the accompanying *Facilitator Notes*, is for family members of those who are incarcerated. It gives family members and returning citizens a common language, learning experience, and plans. Family members can support the returning citizens' 72-Hour Stability Plan to help them through the first crucial hours of their return. Training for GA facilitators will be provided.

    Unique feature: *The Getting Out Model has the capacity to link existing Getting Ahead sites and communities with reentry efforts in those communities. If reentry programs don't exist, the Bridges and GA sites can expand their work to include reentry programming.*

- *The R Rules* by Betti Souther is a two-book set for children of men and women who are incarcerated or in other unstable situations. It would be made available in conjunction with Getting Ahead for family members. Training for facilitators will be provided by aha! Process, Inc.

- *Bridges Out of Poverty* and *Bridges to Sustainable Communities* are books and trainings for community collaboratives to use to address poverty in a comprehensive way. The collaboratives already support GA participants as they stabilize their lives and build their resources—and can extend that support to returning citizens who have used Getting Out to make reentry plans. These collaboratives can either join existing reentry programs or develop reentry programs to support men and women returning from incarceration.

    Unique feature: *Existing Bridges Collaboratives already share the language found in Getting Ahead and Getting Out. They have engaged many sectors in their community to build opportunities for those who are pursuing the goals developed in GA and in Getting Out. The sectors participating in these collaboratives include businesses, employers, healthcare, schools, education, postsecondary education, courts, police, corrections, social services, government, faith-based entities, and early-childhood programs.*

- *Tactical Communication* is a book and training designed for corrections staff, parole and probation officers, police officers, and other first responders so they can understand and apply the concepts found in *Bridges, GA,* and *Getting Out*.

    Unique feature: *Organizations and people from most disciplines can use the core concepts of* Bridges *and the other books to improve their personal skills, their programs, and the outcomes.*

- Reentry programs that meet best-practices criteria can use the Getting Out Model to fill in elements they may not offer—elements such as the pre-release Getting Out or GA for families. Similarly, Bridges Collaboratives need not create a reentry program but can join existing reentry initiatives (see Frequently Asked Questions on next page).

    Unique feature: *The model encourages cooperation with high-quality, existing reentry programs and seeks to find efficiencies that can quickly impact the lives of returning citizens.*

- Support for sites that implement the Getting Out Model includes training for providers; trainer certification for facilitators of Getting Out; informational sessions for sponsors, organizers, and funders; and access to webinars, websites, conferences, newsletters, technical support, and consulting services.

    Getting Out sites are encouraged to participate in the Getting Out Learning Community, which has a website, conference calls, and other opportunities for sharing best practices.

    Unique feature: *The Getting Out Model offers a complete package, rather than a stand-alone model. It encourages collaboration with other reentry programs and community initiatives. The elements described here can be used as a complete set or can be fitted into other high-quality approaches and programs.*

Frequently Asked Questions About the Reentry Model

Who can provide the Getting Out Model?

Getting Ahead while Getting Out can be provided by a correctional facility—or an organization that has the approval of the facility. Getting Out can be offered by organizations that adhere to the Getting Out Model, including Bridges initiatives, reentry programs, faith-based programs, non-governmental organizations, and correctional facilities.

What does it take to get started?

There are four steps in developing a Getting Out Model:

1) Training in the Getting Out Model and the 10 Bridges Out of Poverty Constructs to create a common language for all

2) Embedding, via initial consulting, the concepts into program design and delivery

3) Innovating, evaluating, reflecting, and improving

4) Sharing with other sites (participating in larger Bridges and Getting Ahead Learning Communities)

   1a) Training in the Getting Out Model provided by the authors of *Getting Ahead while Getting Out*:

   Informational sessions on Getting Out Model—one to two hours online and/or onsite for interested people, organizations, institutions, and communities

   Training in Getting Out Model—six hours online and/or onsite for individuals, institutions and communities

   Trainer Certification for Getting Out Facilitators—six hours online and/or onsite

   1b) Training in the 10 Bridges Constructs:

   Training in Bridges Out of Poverty or Bridges to Sustainable Communities for community members, institutions, and reentry providers—six hours by *Getting Ahead while Getting Out* authors or other national Bridges consultants

   Facilitator training for Getting Ahead in a Just-Gettin'-By World—six hours online and/or onsite by author or other national consultant

   Training for correctional staff and/or parole and probation officers based on the book *Tactical Communication*—six hours provided by aha! Process, Inc. consultants

   Training for facilitators of *The R Rules* by author—six hours onsite

2) Embedding and consulting, which are provided by authors of *Getting Ahead while Getting Out,* include:

   Building a reentry program within a Bridges Community Collaborative and/or building partnerships with existing reentry programs that meet best-practices criteria

3) Innovation, evaluation, analysis, and improvement activities include:

   Documentation of activities and decisions of Getting Out Collaborative, analysis of data from web-based providers, maintenance of a continuous quality improvement cycle, and development of new procedures, policies, and programs

4) Sharing with other sites:

   Getting Out Model sites will develop a community of practice to advance learning and share best practices with sites from the U.S. and other countries; activities will include participation in conferences, conference calls, webinars, and online conversations, as well as writing papers and contributing to websites

Which elements should be introduced first?

The goal is to build a complete model. It's logical to build it in phases, starting with the *Getting Ahead while Getting Out* workbook (including facilitator training) and Bridges training in the community as first steps. It's a matter of putting the pieces of the puzzle together to form the whole picture. Some elements need to be developed at the same time, such as trainings in Bridges and/or Tactical Communication for community members and correctional professionals, Getting Out for returning citizens, and GA for their family members.

Do you have to use the whole model?

Yes, but it can be developed in phases, and different groups can provide different elements. An existing reentry program or pre-release program can provide elements of the Getting Out Model to create a complete model. For example, a Bridges initiative might offer the Getting Out and GA elements, whereas a reentry program could provide support for returning citizens—such as access to medication, treatment, transportation, housing, employment, and so on.

Which elements are not essential?

It's not always possible to offer Getting Ahead and The R Rules for the returning citizens' family members. The circumstances are too varied to make that an absolute requirement. For example, family members may not want to be in a GA workshop, or Getting Out participants in a facility may come from a number of communities, making it impractical or impossible to launch GA in each of their communities.

We can't wait for the perfect conditions to offer Getting Out; we must start with the basics and build the model as we go. Henry Ford, the innovator of the automobile assembly line, didn't envision the complete assembly line before he started making cars. He added elements as the need for them arose, inventing solutions as the process unfolded.

What's the ideal approach to a start-up?

There are hundreds of Bridges initiatives in the U.S., Canada, Australia, Czech Republic, Scotland, and Slovakia where Getting Out can be offered in local prisons, jails, and halfway houses. Where there is a fully developed Bridges Collaborative, many of the reentry supports are already in place to support Getting Ahead graduates. Collaboratives often have representatives from many sectors, including colleges/universities, workforce development, courts, employers, early-childhood development, faith-based entities, social services, and treatment facilities.

Similarly there are many reentry programs that already are offering typical support for returning citizens. Most of them can quickly add the Bridges, Getting Ahead, and Getting Out elements to enhance their programming.

What is the role of the correctional facility?

The complete Getting Out Model calls for Getting Out to be offered pre-release. While it's possible for Getting Out to be offered post-release, it's most effective to help those who are incarcerated to take charge of their own plans before reentering their community.

Correctional facilities play a crucial role in making the Getting Out workgroups a success. The buy-in of the warden and his/her staff can make the experience very positive by providing a safe and neutral learning environment. The training provided by the facilities for volunteers and professionals is crucial to the effectiveness and safety of the experience for all concerned.

What does it take to become a Certified Facilitator for Getting Ahead while Getting Out?

Two-year certifications and Lifetime Certification options are available.

The prerequisites for attending a certification training:

- Attend a Bridges Out of Poverty Day One training either in person or through the audio workshop
- Read the *Getting Ahead while Getting Out* workbook and the accompanying *User Guide* (the resource you are now reading)

The certification process includes:

- Attending a six-hour online Facilitator Training or an onsite Facilitator Training
- Online recertification, which is required every two years for those who do not have Lifetime Certification
- Lifetime Certification, which includes free online sessions

How does Getting Out work with existing reentry programs?

Getting Out is designed to fit into existing reentry programs that meet best-practices criteria.

What role does the community play?

- Catalyst—someone to introduce the Getting Out Model to the community, institutions, and potential partners; it is someone who is attracted to Bridges and Getting Out who can engage others from the community
- Organizer—an individual or organization with the passion and ability to build and organize the Getting Out initiative
- Members, individuals, and organizations that are attracted to the Getting Out Model and committed to helping returning citizens reenter the community
- Funders, individuals, and organizations that can invest in the initiative and encourage others to invest as well
- Trainers and facilitators who are passionate, willing to be trained, and effective communicators
- Those who provide support and programming to returning citizens at the individual and organizational levels
- Those who educate the community in general and employers specifically about the needs of returning citizens and the importance of this program to the community

What is the minimum training needed for community volunteers and agency staff?

- Attend a Bridges Out of Poverty or Tactical Communication workshop
- To facilitate Getting Out, one must become a Certified Facilitator of Getting Out by attending an online or onsite training
- Must attend all trainings for volunteers and providers required by the correctional facility and comply with all rules and regulations

What reentry programs can Getting Out initiatives collaborate with?

We recommend these best-practices criteria established by the Eisenhower Foundation—Reentry Programs for Previously Incarcerated Persons (prepared by LaFrance Associates, LLC). The program must:

- Have been or be in the process of conducting outcome evaluations
- Serve previously incarcerated persons as its primary population
- Meet multiple needs of previously incarcerated persons
- Provide pre-release programming and post-release support
- Provide or be able to refer investigators to mental health and substance abuse treatment
- Focus on motivation, envision new roles and self-concepts, and nurture the commitment to change

- Offer support and immediate access to income in the days following release
- Look for compatibilities between individuals' temperaments and available jobs
- Provide non-punitive, problem-solving assistance
- Develop resources for or provide access to concrete supports like transportation, interviewing skills, work clothes, childcare, housing, and food
- Create a well-developed network of potential employers
- Cultivate employer satisfaction through frequent contact and willingness to mediate conflicts
- Coordinate employment and criminal justice commitments to provide as little disruption to job responsibilities as possible
- Focus on job retention
- Take place in community settings (as opposed to institutions)
- Be intensive and offer services for at least six months
- Use cognitive-behavioral treatment techniques, which involve defining problems that led to conflicts with the law/authorities, selecting goals, generating a plan to meet goals, and implementing solutions
- Use praise and reward as generally outweighing punishments and other punitive measures
- Provide previously incarcerated persons with vocational training and job-enhancing opportunities

Also recommended:

- Meet the Big 4 Criminogenic Needs
  - Anti-social cognition
  - Anti-social companions
  - Anti-social personality/temperament
  - Family and/or marital disruption
- Meet the Lesser 4 Criminogenic Needs
  - Substance abuse
  - Employment
  - Education
  - Leisure and/or recreation

Source: D. A. Andrews and J. Bonta, *The Psychology of Criminal Conduct*, 2010.

Data Collection, Evaluations, Reports, and Social Media

Collecting data, evaluating our work, and doing research are absolutely necessary for these reasons:

- Improvement in design, delivery, and effectiveness of GA
- Reporting to funders and community
- Grant awards
- Ongoing support for GA grads and individuals challenged by resource instability
- Spreading the work to new communities and sites

The purpose of this section is to describe the evaluation instruments and clarify the options. We are using tables to cut down on text. Key elements can be seen at a glance. Within each table is a bit of information about each of the providers, their products, and contact info. Go to these links to learn more about the products and to contact the providers.

Here are the four tools:

- St. Joseph County (IN) evaluation tool for pre/post feedback on Getting Ahead effectiveness
- Charity Tracker cloud-based shared case management framework with *integrated* evaluation tools to collect longer-term results for GA participants
- Beacon mobile app—personal support tools for GA grads
- MPOWR web-based case management and community collaboration tools based on 15 areas of life

1. **Evaluation Tool for Pre/Post Feedback on Getting Ahead Effectiveness:** GA sites need to be able to demonstrate the effectiveness of the program in order to share with funders and to improve their delivery of the program. This pre/post assessment, which fits the philosophy and purpose of GA, meets that need.

		Getting Ahead Pre/Post Assessment—Pre/Post Feedback on Group		
Instrument	**Provider**	**Elements**	**Cost**	**Action/Opportunity**
Pre/Post Getting Ahead Class Assessment	St. Joseph County (IN) Bridges Out of Poverty Initiative	Pre/post feedback available a month after graduation of each GA group 1. Demographic profile of the GA class 2. Percentage of change on 35 items to measure motivation, self-efficacy, content knowledge, self-reflexivity, and hope 3. Percentage of change on four items measuring participants' perceptions of poverty 4. A qualitative section demonstrating changes in participants' goals, dreams, personal strategies for Getting Ahead, and perceptions of self 5. A 14-point evaluation of class from participants' perspectives, providing feedback to assist your agency in improving Getting Ahead	$250 per group	Contact: Executive Director St. Joseph County Bridges Out of Poverty Initiative P.O. Box 1078 South Bend, IN 46628 (574) 339-1232 (cell) or (574) 246-0533 SJCBridges@gmail.com *www.SJCBridges.org*

2. **Charity Tracker PLUS Cloud-Based Evaluation Tools to Assess Getting Ahead Effectiveness:** Track model fidelity, stability, resource development, and ROI (return on investment) elements embedded with case management. Getting Ahead sites need to document and report on the improvement in stability and the development of resources of GA graduates.

Cloud-Based Evaluation Tools in Case Management Frame				
Instrument	**Provider**	**Elements**	**Cost**	**Action/Opportunity**
Charity Tracker PLUS Getting Ahead Assessment * Modules to assess stability, resource development, ROI items, and model fidelity elements Available to all Bridges Charity Tracker subscribers, all-inclusive	Simon Solutions, Inc. Easy-to-use, cloud-based service used by churches, charities, and entire communities (752 cities) to maximize efficiency while helping others ~Case management bulletins, alerts, and referrals ~Outcomes ~File uploads ~Barcode ~Scanning ~Services index ~Reports and statistics	Demographics and baseline assessment data collected during GA class (Module 8), then in chosen incremental time periods, such as three-month, or semi-annual, or annual intervals after GA graduation User enters data and runs standard reports as needed De-identified (no names or personal data included) results provided to aha! Process to be aggregated with national data (for users following model); aggregated data will be shared with all users Elements of evaluation ~Self-assessment of 11 resources ~5-Point Stability Scale ~Return on investment: income, debt, assets, and benefits ~Model Fidelity elements for user organizations	$25/month, per user * Elements available to Bridges subscribers, all-inclusive Volume discount pricing available, starting with 10+ users	CharityTracker *www.CharityTracker.com* Contact: Joey Yarber, Sales/Implementation (888) 764-0633 info@charitytracker.com

3. **Web and Mobile App Tools for Getting Ahead Grads:** We have long sought to find new and effective ways to continue to support GA grads after they have completed the Getting Ahead sessions. These tools are for personal use and are targeted primarily toward GA grads.

Getting Ahead Mobile App and Web-Based Conferencing				
Instrument	Provider	Elements	Cost	Action/Opportunity
GA app, daily personal support for GA grads' stability and resource development	Beacon Voice, LLC	Daily personal support for GA grads as they track the development of stability and the 11 Bridges Resources Features include: 1. Trend lines for each stability indicator and resource 2. Identification of social connections, local supports, and websites 3. Identification of immediate action to be taken 4. Documentation using stories and photos	Free to GA graduates	Contact Beacon Voice: sam@beaconvoice.com *www.beaconvoice.com* To order: Google Play
Getting Ahead Network Conference Room	Moderators: David Walker, Amber Werner, and Michelle Wood	Getting Ahead Network has online conference room where GA graduates can meet for conversations.	Free	Contact: davidwalker@oneroadsupport.org A new initiative, in the experimental phase, to bring GA grads from across the United States together

4. MPOWR Web-Based Case Management and Community Collaboration Tools: Track model fidelity, stability, resource development, and ROI (return on investment) elements embedded with case management. Getting Ahead sites and Bridges Communities may want to offer case-management services for GA grads and/or use data systems to build community collaboratives.

Web-Based Case Management and Community Collaboration Tools

Instrument	Provider	Elements	Cost	Action/Opportunity
MPOWR "Full Case Management System"	SupplyCore, Inc.	MPOWR is a comprehensive participant-centered community case management system that facilitates inter-agency client assessment, goal setting, and resource coordination for all areas of life. Growing community collaborations and statewide initiatives will require the maturity, flexibility, and proprietary HIPAA-compliant data sharing Release of Information model available only through MPOWR, which also can provide data-integration services to coordinate with existing data systems.	$50 per user per month (Additional $600 one time agency set-up fee and $600 annual agency maintenance fee)	Contact Brooke Saucier, manager of Partnership Programs, to schedule a demo and get a full pricing scenario for your planned coalition. brooke.saucier@supplycore.com (815) 997-1660 Also see MPOWR website at: *www.mpowr.com*
MPOWR *Stand-alone* "Getting Ahead Module" with Stability Scale	SupplyCore, Inc.	MPOWR *Stand-alone* GA Module will provide MPOWR and non-MPOWR GA sites all they need to run and monitor GA classes, including: • A GA Classroom Module to record attendance • A Demographics Tab to record participant demographic information • An 11 Resources Tab to monitor participant progress in development of 11 resources • A GA Assessment Tab to record GA class assessments at standard intervals, compiling scores from 11-resource sub-tabs and graphing results • 5-point Stability Scale • Standard Reports to report on local, regional, and national GA data; shared with aha! Process will be deidentified data (unlinkable) and aggregated data will be shared with users.	$200 per GA class (Additional $400 one-time GA site set-up fee)	Contact Brooke Saucier, manager of Partnership Programs, to schedule a demo and get a full pricing scenario for your planned coalition. brooke.saucier@supplycore.com (815) 997-1660 Also see MPOWR website at: *www.mpowr.com* * See book *Bridges to Wholeness: Using MPOWR, a data-driven collaborative model for addressing poverty and related social issues;* available through aha! Process.

How Getting Out Fits into Bridges Initiatives

As noted in the section on the Getting Out Reentry Model, the families of returning citizens and the returning citizen themselves can benefit from GA support system that can be found in Bridges Communities.

Bridges initiatives are built on the principle of attraction. Those who like Bridges concepts enough to act on them will typically want to engage people from poverty by offering Getting Ahead. Bonnie Bazata from the St. Joseph Bridges Out of Poverty Initiative (IN) says, "GA is the high-octane fuel in the tank. It is the piece that will drive this [Bridges initiative] forward."

Bridges initiatives typically begin with a number of Bridges workshops. Those workshops identify funders, sponsors, and facilitators for GA. They also produce the support structures that GA grads will use to help them make the transition out of poverty.

People in poverty become the center of the work. By joining the initiative, they provide vital information about poverty and the barriers to transition that middle-class people may not know about. By taking a seat at the planning and decision-making tables, they make sure the work is relevant for those in poverty or in unstable lives.

Without GA grads at the table, the initiatives are more likely to revert to the dominance and "righting reflex" of the middle class. People who come together across class lines to solve problems are a unique feature of Bridges initiatives.

GA groups contribute the following to the initiative:

- GA investigators provide the community with an accurate Mental Model of Poverty in their particular community.
- Investigators provide an assessment of the community.
- Investigators identify barriers to transition.
- Investigators identify solutions.

In the future it may be possible for GA grads to be surveyed for information on pending legislation and community, state, or national issues. GA grads have a way of analyzing and speaking to poverty issues that includes:

- An understanding of class issues and the hidden rules of class that gives them a voice and power
- A definition of poverty that can test proposals for how well resources are built
- An understanding of the causes of poverty that helps test if all causes are addressed
- The 10 Bridges Constructs by which to test the efficacy of proposals (see Appendix I in the *Getting Ahead while Getting Out* workbook).

One of the unique features of Bridges and Getting Ahead is the thousands of people who share a common language and set of constructs for poverty, prosperity, and sustainability issues. That network is a largely untapped source of knowledge and influence.

The Community

We need to know how Getting Out can fit into the array of programs and activities in a community.

Providers of services for people in poverty and returning citizens fall into one or more of five groups: federal and state government agencies, non-profit organizations, for-profit entities, grassroots organizations, and community collaboratives.

The subgroups under these five don't line up neatly. For example, faith-based organizations may fit under non-profits or grassroots organizations. It can get confusing when non-profits and for-profits deliver services using government funds. An example would be a faith-based hospital (non-profit) that delivers services using federal dollars. Another would be the for-profit prisons that receive public funds.

Getting Ahead Sites

Casinos	Food pantries	Mobile home parks
Circles of Support	Foster programs	Native American communities
Community Action Agencies	Goodwill Industries	Prisons
Community centers	Habitat for Humanity	Residential treatment
Community colleges	Head Start	Roma communities (Slovakia)
Crisis centers	Healthcare providers	Schools (parents)
Domestic violence shelters	High schools (students)	Section 8 housing
Drug courts	Homeless shelters	Universities
Early-childhood centers	Hospitals	Workforce development
Faith-based initiatives	Jails	Workplace/employers
Family courts	Mental health centers	YMCA/YWCA

Circles, Foster Care, Prison, and the Workplace

As an agenda-free learning experience, Getting Ahead is designed to be used in any setting. The assumption is that GA grads will determine what their future story is. That would be their agenda: physical well-being, financial literacy, work readiness, community college, jobs, etc. The sponsors also would build follow-up supports and activities for graduates.

Sometimes, however, Getting Ahead is sponsored by an organization that *wants* something of the investigators after they complete GA. Those expectations are usually transparent or self-evident. Drug courts want offenders to establish a sober and drug-free life. Circles initiatives want investigators to become Circle Leaders. Foster-care programs want young people to emancipate successfully to adulthood. Prisons want offenders to integrate successfully into society and not reoffend. Employers want investigators to perform their jobs well and keep those jobs for years.

In all of these cases the goal of the sponsor can be an addition to the future-story plans developed by the investigator. For example, GA investigators in a drug court are expected to get clean and sober. Getting Ahead can help support a person's recovery, going beyond the issues of addiction, to build other resources for a higher quality of life.

In those cases the mission or agenda is positive. The investigator would value becoming a Circle Leader, leaving the foster-care system successfully, staying out of prison, and/or keeping a job.

Subtle as it may seem, however, adding an agenda may matter to the facilitator and the investigators. The danger is that the message to the investigators may change in these ways:

Agenda-Free	Agenda
You are a problem solver.	You need to do what we have prepared for you.
Choose the changes you want to make.	Change in this direction, in this way.
You will figure out what you need to do in order to connect the dots in your own way.	We will connect the dots for you.
You will be in charge of your learning.	We will teach.

Getting Ahead works because it is agenda-free; adding an agenda can change the learning dynamic that makes Getting Ahead unique. Knowing that, how can Getting Ahead be provided in specific settings like those mentioned and still retain its key features?

Create a firewall to protect the integrity of the Getting Ahead model by naming the mission, agenda, and expectations of the sponsor when recruiting. That way the investigators know what is expected of them when they agree to participate.

Support from aha! Process

Facilitators need to know how Getting Ahead (and Investigations into Economic Class in America) fit into all the initiatives and products under the aha! Process umbrella.

The Bridges Continuum is used by communities to develop a comprehensive approach to poverty. It illustrates these points:

1. Looking at the headings across the top of the chart, one can see that poverty must be addressed at all stages of life.
   a. Birth to 6: Getting Ahead can be offered to parents at early-childhood centers and Early Head Start. In Getting Ahead, investigations are made into language experience and brain development, mediation, and the value of building social capital with schools.
   b. K–12: GA is offered to parents and, in some cases, high school juniors and seniors. This is typically done over the course of a school year and is coupled with *The R Rules* by Betti Souther. *The R Rules* is designed for students from eighth grade to age 19. It is a collection of youth-oriented activities that illustrate the concepts in Bridges and Getting Ahead.
   c. Postsecondary: Many first-generation, low-income students at trade schools, technical schools, community colleges, and universities are now using the *Investigations into Economic Class in America* workbook.
   d. Three columns about work and careers: Some employers use Getting Ahead to help investigators/employees improve their attendance and move up to better paying jobs.
   e. Wellness: This column includes areas of life having to do with physical health, emotional well-being, social capital, and all other issues covered by local agencies and organizations.
   f. Communities: GA graduates participate in planning and decision making.

2. There's a role for everyone in the community. Each group and sector can use Bridges and Getting Ahead in its own institutions to improve outcomes.
   a. It's important that each organization benefit by using Bridges and Getting Ahead.
   b. We recognize that GA grads can benefit too if there's an intention on the part of those organizations (technical schools, employers, schools) to welcome and support GA grads.
   c. It's important that the organizations and sectors meet to learn from each other, collaborate on initiatives, and address systemic issues that impact GA grads and others in poverty.
   d. When all the organizations that use Framework, Bridges, and Getting Ahead come together, they can operate above the institutional, professional, and agency "silos."

3. There are many products, initiatives, and trainers at aha! Process that can enhance the work.
   a. This gives everyone a common language and set of constructs.
   b. A community of practice that includes the local community and aha! Process can establish ways to evaluate the work and support one another.

The Bridges Continuum creates critical mass; more and more people use the ideas. This can lead to many new applications and more support for people who are making the transition out of poverty.

Getting Ahead fits best in a community where there's a Bridges collaborative made up of several institutions that have applied Bridges concepts.

THE BRIDGES CONTINUUM
COMPREHENSIVE STRATEGIES FOR BRIDGES STEERING COMMITTEES

	Pre-conception to 6	K–12	Postsecondary	Workforce Prep/ Placement
Metrics: Ending Poverty Scorecard	Ready for school Language experience, brain development, cognitive learning structures	Graduation rates GEDs	Retention rates Graduation rates Certifications	Employment rate Apprenticeships Certifications Availability of jobs Mix of jobs
Fallout Costs	Failure to act here means giving up the highest returns on dollars spent on interventions; for birth to 5 the returns can be as high as 15–17%.[i]	Dropouts from the class of 2007 will cost the U.S. nearly $329 billion in lost wages, taxes, and productivity in their lifetimes.[ii]	Loss of income: lifetime earnings of a male with a bachelor's degree in 2004 were 96% higher than a male with a high school diploma.[iii]	Crime imposes costs of as much as $1–2 trillion per year. The savings that can be realized by preventing crime and delinquency among youths are extremely high.[iv]
Family of Strategies Using aha! Process Constructs	*Tucker Signing Strategies Reading by Age 5* Getting Ahead with parents Develop an early-childhood champion Bridges Early Childhood Community of Practice	Ruby Payne schools— Framework training *The R Rules Collaboration For Kids* Dropout prevention Financial literacy	*Investigations into Economic Class in America Understanding and Engaging Under-Resourced College Students* Achievement Alliance Community of Practice	Cascade Engineering/Quest Cincinnati Works The Source Getting Ahead Future Story Project, IN Bridges Business Community of Practice
Who Takes Responsibility for Change	Families, early-childhood development field	Parents, students, educators, school boards, PTAs, taxpayers	Students, faculty, administrators, boards, communities, benefactors	Employers, employees, government, colleges, chambers of commerce, economic and community developers, workforce development, high schools

[i] Heckman, James J. "Investing in Disadvantaged Young Children is an Economically Efficient Policy." Paper presented at Committee for Economic Development, the Pew Charitable Trusts, PNC Financial Services Group Forum on "Building the Economic Case for Investments in Preschool." New York, January 10, 2006.
[ii] High School Dropouts in America, Alliance for Excellent Education, http://www.all4ed.org/files/GraduationRates_FactSheet.pdf
[iii] Kirsch, Irwin, Braun, Henry, & Yamamoto, Kentaro. (January 2007). "America's Perfect Storm: Three Forces Changing Our Nation's Future." Princeton, NJ: Educational Testing Service.
[iv] Holzer, Harry J. "Workforce Development and the Disadvantaged." The Urban Institute, Brief 7, September 2008. www.urban.org/UploadPDF/411761_workforce_development.PDF

Source: Adapted by Scott Miller (Move the Mountain, Inc.) and Philip DeVol (aha! Process, Inc.).

Prepared by Scott Miller of Move the Mountain, Inc.
and Philip DeVol of aha! Process, Inc.

www.ahaprocess.com
www.movethemountain.org
© 2009 by aha! Process, Inc.
© 2009 Move the Mountain, Inc.

Job Retention	Self-Sufficient Income	Seniors	Wellness	Community Prosperity
One-year minimum	Self-sufficient wage (Wider Opportunities for Women) 200% poverty guidelines goals met for households Assets established	Poverty rate Access to housing and healthcare	High resources—all 11 Balanced life Giving back to the community	Environmental sustainability Economic viability where everyone can live well Low rates of poverty and disparity Social Health Indices are positive
$5,505.08 average turnover cost for an $8 an hour employee[v]	Children who live in families with an annual income less than $15,000 are 22 times more likely to be abused or neglected than children living in families with an annual income of $30,000 or more.[vi]	Individuals 55 and older accounted for 22% of all personal bankruptcies in 2007, compared with 8% in 1991. Healthcare costs proved to be the top reason for many of these bankruptcies.[vii]	Poor rankings in the OECD (Organisation for Economic Co-operation and Development)[viii]	Persistent childhood poverty is estimated to cost our nation $500 billion a year, or about 4% of GDP.[ix] Communities that have lost manufacturing jobs, businesses, and their tax base are not viable economically and socially.
Cascade Engineering/Quest Cincinnati Works The Source Getting Ahead for new employees Working Bridges Employer Workgroup, Vermont Bridges Business Community of Practice	Employer in-house advancement strategies Bridges training Cascade Engineering/Quest Cincinnati Works The Source Bridges Business Community of Practice	Wider Opportunities for Women	Comprehensive delivery systems SupplyCore Technology Group's MPOWR program Bridges to Health Community of Practice *Tactical Communication* Bridges Criminal Justice Community of Practice	Bridges Steering Committees Community Sustainability Grid Systemic change and policy issues sectors Circles Campaign Bridges Communities of Practice
Employers, employees, chambers of commerce, economic and community developers, workforce development, human services, government	Policymakers, employers, employees, workforce development, government, human services	Service providers, faith community, government, neighborhood associations, civic groups	Faith community, civic organizations, medical community, law enforcement, neighborhood associations, political parties	Bridges Steering Committees, people and organizations from all other points on the continuum. People from all classes, races, and political persuasions

[v] Compilation of Turnover Studies, SASHA Corporation, http://www.sashacorp.com/turnframe.html
[vi] American Humane, http://www.americanhumane.org/about-us/newsroom/fact-sheets/americas-children.html
[vii] Health Care Costs, Economy Pushing Senior Citizens to Bankruptcy and Poverty in the U.S., Senior Journal.com. http://seniorjournal.com/NEWS/SeniorStats/2008/20080826-USSeniorCitizensInPoverty.htm
[viii] Burd-Sharps, Sarah, et al. (2008). The Measure of America: American Human Development Report 2008-2009. New York, NY: Columbia University Press.
[ix] Center for American Progress, From Poverty to Prosperity: A National Strategy to Cut Poverty in Half, April 2007. www.americanprogress.org/issues/2007/04/pdf/poverty_report.pdf

Getting Ahead: What It's About

Support for GA Graduates

The hard work begins after the investigators celebrate at their graduation ceremony. This is when the investigators begin working on their future stories. It's vital that people from all classes who are invested in a Bridges and Getting Ahead initiative share a common language and vision. Given the complexities of our work, it's easy to act out of old ways of thinking. The following unique features can help keep the vision crystal clear.

2. Unique Features of Bridges Structures and Operations

UNIQUE FEATURES	BRIEF EXPLANATIONS
Bridges is a set of concepts, strategies, and tools, as well as a language; it is not a program.	People, organizations, and communities use Bridges to make their programs better, to get improved outcomes.
Bridges operates under the principles of attraction and ownership.	Those attracted to Bridges are encouraged to take ownership of the ideas and apply them in their own organizations and communities.
Bridges operates above the silos/departmental thinking.	Organizations can use Bridges to improve their outcomes, but when people come to Bridges Steering Committees, they leave their silos at the door and focus on how to help people make the transition out of poverty.
Bridges is applied locally according to the history, leadership, best practices, and unique characteristics of the organization and community.	Bridges recommends principles but doesn't impose programs and strategies; it isn't "one size fits all."
Bridges encourages innovation based on the Core Constructs and principles of Bridges.	Bridges has an evolving community of practice where organizations and communities share knowledge with each other at the local, sector, national, and international levels.
Bridges is a form of participatory action research (PAR).	Participants review their work and adapt and improve their models accordingly.
Bridges is a form of participatory democracy.	Communities come together to solve problems; they don't wait for the "authority" to act.

continued on next page

continued from previous page

2. Unique Features of Bridges Structures and Operations

UNIQUE FEATURES	BRIEF EXPLANATIONS
Bridges helps develop sophisticated service delivery systems.	Communities that embrace Bridges can reorganize to focus on helping people get out of poverty.
Bridges is a community engagement model.	Bridges helps design pathways to economic self-sufficiency and well-rounded lives by engaging the business, educational, faith, and civic sectors.
Bridges uses the hidden rules of class to bring people together across class lines to solve community problems.	Bridges raises class issues in order to help people form relationships of mutual respect across class lines, as a way of solving problems.
Bridges promotes sustainable communities where everyone can live well.	Communities often define themselves in such a way that they leave out people in poverty and award a sustainable life to their own circle or class.

Investigators' Initiatives—Support for Each Other

We've learned a lot about how to support GA graduates since 2004. As the number of communities and organizations using GA has grown, a spontaneous learning community sprang up. This took the form of Bridges Institutes, which has now morphed into an annual conference that attracts hundreds of people from all classes and many sectors. These people come together from the United States and other countries to share their innovations and best practices.

3. Unique Features of Community Support Based on Bridges Model

UNIQUE FEATURES	BRIEF EXPLANATIONS
Getting Ahead graduates are at the center of community initiatives.	Bridges initiatives are kept relevant by attending to the information, insights, and solutions provided by GA graduates.
The learning for people from all classes deepens as GA graduates make the transition out of poverty.	Getting Ahead is part of the broader Bridges initiative that provides the same language and constructs to people in our institutions and communities.
Getting Ahead graduates take their seat at the planning and decision-making tables in the community.	GA graduates participate in the development of programs, policies, and products that have to do with poverty and community sustainability.

continued on next page

continued from previous page

3. Unique Features of Community Support Based on Bridges Model

UNIQUE FEATURES	BRIEF EXPLANATIONS
Institutions and communities organize long-term support for GA graduates.	Sponsors of GA keep the promise that is implied by all programs that are designed for people in poverty: "By coming here things will be better for you." That promise is broken all too often by organizations that don't take the long view.
Bridges initiatives support the self-organizing approaches and structures developed by GA graduates.	Bridging social capital, developed during and after GA, is often the first and strongest support for change.
Bridges initiatives provide long-term support for transition.	Innovative ways of providing support are being developed by Bridges, Circles, and other local and national organizations.
Bridges initiatives bring all sectors to the table and operate without the silos.	The concepts, tools, and strategies provided by Bridges can help develop community engagement models.
Bridges concepts are being used by a number of sectors (business, postsecondary, K–12, health, criminal justice, early childhood, etc.) that help GA graduates build resources.	The more sectors in the community that apply Bridges concepts, the broader and sturdier the bridge out of poverty.
Bridges initiatives engage people from all classes, races, sectors, and political persuasions.	Bridges has the tools to attract these people and bring them together to work on building resources with those in poverty.
Bridges is a learning community that gives power and voice to GA graduates.	The communities of practice—or learning communities—are continually developing new strategies and programs. Bridges uses technology, social capital, and a national conference to share best practices.
Bridges and Getting Ahead help people understand their own economic and societal experiences. This provides a better understanding of those in other economic classes.	Typically the person from middle class learns about people from poverty in order to help them improve their circumstances. This usually is accomplished through the expectation that the thinking or attitude of the person in poverty will change. In Bridges and Getting Ahead, the changes in thinking and attitude take place in people from all classes.
Bridges and Getting Ahead promote sustainable communities where everyone can live well.	Poverty is too costly to people in poverty and to society—in terms of both the wasted potential of people and the cost to society of living in economic enclaves.

Our rapidly expanding learning community has a lot to offer new sites. Even so, we're still in the learning and innovation stage. There are three groups, actors, or entities that provide support:

1. GA investigators themselves

2. Community collaboratives, such as Bridges Steering Committees (which go by various names) and Guiding Coalitions associated with Circle sites

3. Organizations that sponsor Getting Ahead

While reading about the following approaches, keep these general guidelines in mind:

- There must be something already in place to support graduates before you complete the first GA group. This doesn't mean the entire initiative has to be set up and functioning before you begin, but it's essential that all the key partners are fully Bridges-trained.

- Every community is different. This section will give you an idea of the range of options. Do some follow-up research using the links provided in Appendix 8 and develop an approach that fits your local situation.

- Who the catalysts are, what resources are available, and the history of collaboration will determine the quality of support GA graduates will receive.
  - All three of the approaches listed above are valuable and can work in conjunction with one another.
  - There are many examples and models that can inform local planners. You're encouraged to visit the many websites devoted to the application of Bridges and Getting Ahead.

GA graduates consistently report that the very first support they get is from each other. This begins while they're still in Getting Ahead and continues afterward. Graduates report that, in the short time they're in Getting Ahead, they get to know other investigators at an even deeper level than some of their lifelong friends.

In *Bowling Alone* (2000), Robert Putnam writes about social capital by region and state in the U.S. He says,

… the level of informal social capital in the state is a stronger predictor of student achievement than is the formal institutionalized social capital. In other words, the level of social trust in a state and the frequency with which people connected informally with one another (in card games, visiting with friends, and the like) were even more closely correlated with educational performance than was the amount of time state residents devoted to club meetings, church attendance, and community projects." (p. 300)

1. GA grads develop informal and formal support

   - During and after Getting Ahead, investigators provide each other with resources like childcare, transportation, food, and social connections.

   - In Northeast Colorado's frontier counties some groups continued to gather around the kitchen table, bringing potluck dishes to each other's homes.

   - Some groups have met to review their plans, redo their self-assessment to check their progress, and update their future-story mental models.

   - One investigator started a "Budgeting Group" that meets monthly.

   - GA and Investigations graduates formed the Youngstown (OH) State University Bridges Out of Poverty Student Union. They work with colleges within the university to help provide a good experience for students from poverty; supply speakers to local agencies; speak at conferences; and even lobby in Washington, DC.

   - In Longview, TX, the Bridges Buddies group organizes regular meetings for fellow GA graduates.

   - GA graduates help organize and run the support programs offered by sponsors of Getting Ahead.

   - As noted above, GA grads speak at conferences, serve on panels, and do volunteer work.

- GA grads become GA facilitators.

- Getting Ahead investigators and graduates, including ex-offenders, helped with the development of *Investigations into Economic Class in America* and this book.

- When investigators take the lead in building support systems and in contributing to solutions, it is the essence of the Getting Ahead philosophy. Sponsors and facilitators who learn from and take direction from GA grads as peers are fulfilling their truest role.

2. Stability and resource development: exceptions to the rule

    GA graduates are teaching us the subtleties and nuances of what it means to build resources and move out of poverty. Stability and building resources can mean different things to different individuals. We know that stability is generally a positive thing and that too much instability can lead to a life in the tyranny of the moment. But we also know that poverty itself can be *stable*. GA graduates explain that leaving what you know for what you don't know causes instability. It also challenges one's sense of self, one's identity.

Building resources doesn't immediately or automatically stabilize a person's situation. This process can cause instability in very specific ways. For example, giving up subsidized housing (which feels so secure) in order to pursue a better paying job is a risky move. There's no guarantee that the job will always be there or that housing costs won't rise. As one GA grad put it, "Stepping from the safety net to the ladder is very shaky."

We also assume that higher resources are generally a positive thing. But we should be conscious that there are exceptions to the rule. A Native American couple explained why they *embrace* poverty and do not choose higher financial resources that could provide such things as running water and electricity. In order to build those resources, as a tribe they would have to give up tribal ownership of the land for private or individual ownership. They know that some individuals would sell their land and the beautiful landscape would then be covered with gas stations and strip malls. The stability they value is the land as it is; building their financial resources would bring about instability.

Indeed, some individuals and groups choose to live simply; some strive to have a small carbon footprint. For some people having a high quality of life means choosing a life with fewer amenities and not being a "mad consumer."

Issues that arise when you begin to make changes: time and identity

Some people dramatically change the way they spend time. One graduate said she no longer drifts through weekends. Instead of spending the entire weekend with friends and then missing a college class on Monday morning, she now visits with friends for two hours and never misses a class.

How time is spent changes too. What you do with your friends, what you talk about, may not be as satisfying as it once was. Negativity no longer satisfies; positive action does.

This shift in the use of time leads to a shift in identity. When self-image changes, it can be stressful because a new identity is being formed. But it isn't fully in place yet. Processing the change with people who are on the same journey is what informal support systems can provide.

Getting Ahead: What It's About

Community Models That Benefit GA Graduates

The following descriptions are very brief. The rate at which communities are innovating and building new programs and approaches will soon outdate this book. For up-to-date descriptions, go to their websites listed in Appendix 8.

1. The St. Joseph County Bridges Out of Poverty Initiative in South Bend, IN, is a non-profit organization set up to address poverty in a comprehensive way. It began to organize in 2004 and, after a number of Bridges workshops, began offering Getting Ahead. It supports organizations that sponsor Getting Ahead. The organization doesn't deliver services, but focuses on systemic and policy-level changes in several sectors, leaving the management of programs and services to existing agencies. The features of their model are:

   a. A monthly networking meeting that brings GA grads together with middle-class allies to review Bridges concepts, identify barriers to transition in the community, and find solutions.

   b. The Future Story Project that links GA graduates to employers and assists those employers in applying Bridges concepts in their organizations.

   c. Engaging the postsecondary world. The South Bend group was the first organization to assist a college (Ivy Tech Community College) in offering Getting Ahead. A high percentage of GA grads are now students on that campus.

   d. A hospital is using Bridges concepts to improve retention rates of employees and enhance patient care.

   e. A financial literacy course for GA grads, with assistance in developing non-financial resources as well.

   f. Maintaining a focus on systemic issues, such as transportation problems in the city.

> 'The course starts with a huge reality check that forms an understanding in the group. "My life now" isn't "How it has to be." Realizing that I have the power to make my life go up or go down made the rest of the information relevant. Then I learned how to use it.'
>
> —Brandy Bates, College Student, Youngstown (OH) State University Bridges Out of Poverty Student Union

2. Circles of Support: Community Action Duluth's [MN] Community Engagement Strategy offers Getting Ahead, which is described as a 20-session interactive leadership development program for low-income people with a non-traditional volunteer support to single mothers, the majority of whom are people of color. In addition, they convene workshops to educate middle-class allies about the impact of systemic class and structural racism. Last but most importantly, they host a monthly community forum called Big View that incorporates a quarterly presentation called Solutions to End Poverty. Their strategy is designed to bring people together across race and class lines to advance equity, fairness, and openness while addressing concerns that impact people who live in poverty.

3. A scan of the Bridges and Getting Ahead websites will lead to additional approaches and strategies (many of these websites are listed in Appendix 8). This is a period of innovation, not just for Bridges and Getting Ahead, but for many groups that focus on poverty, quality of life, and sustainability issues. Communities are encouraged to seek out best practices that are consistent with Getting Ahead and Bridges principles.

Institutional and Sector Approaches That Benefit GA Graduates

Corporations and the Business Sector

As more and more institutions began to apply Bridges concepts, new learning communities formed. The first business to use Bridges concepts was Cascade Engineering, a plastics firm in Grand Rapids, MI (1999). Cascade Engineering developed an in-house approach and a partnership with public-sector organizations that improved its retention rates dramatically.

Cincinnati Works developed an Employee Assistance Program model for low-wage workers in Cincinnati, OH. Cascade Engineering and Cincinnati Works served as models for innovations like Working Bridges in Vermont, The Source in Michigan, and the Future Story Project in South Bend, IN. Hospitals have used Getting Ahead to improve retention rates of new hires and to help their employees climb the ladder to better paying jobs.

> 'Bonding social capital is good for "getting by," but bridging social capital is good for "getting ahead."'
>
> –Xavier de Souza Briggs,
> U.S. Sociologist and Planner

All of the business initiatives have improved the company's bottom line, as well as their reputations in the community. But GA graduates and others from poverty and incarceration gain. They benefit in direct ways when they get jobs with companies that have applied Bridges concepts. GA graduates and others from poverty and incarceration benefit in a general way because of the change in the mindset and culture at the business sites. It broadens the bridge out of poverty.

Postsecondary Sector

A growing number of technical schools, community colleges, colleges, and universities are using concepts from Ruby Payne's *A Framework for Understanding Poverty* and *Bridges Out of Poverty* to improve the academic performance of first-generation, low-income students, as well as to improve retention and graduation rates.

Their primary tools are two recently published aha! Process books: *Understanding and Engaging Under-Resourced College Students* and *Investigations into Economic Class in America*. The *Investigations* book is the postsecondary version of Getting Ahead. It received the 2011 Distinguished Achievement Award in the Curriculum—Adult Life Skills category and was also a finalist for the 2011 Golden Lamp Award and the 2011 Innovation Award by the Association of Educational Publishers.

College Achievement Alliance (see next page), a campus strategy from *Understanding and Engaging Under-Resourced College Students,* is a campus and community support system for first-generation, low-income students (particularly those who are Investigations graduates) that helps them stay on campus quarter by quarter until they graduate.

The sections above and below the circles name the external and internal stakeholders. These are the two worlds that college students navigate at the same time. At the center of this approach are the student investigators. The circle surrounding them shows the activities and goals of campus life.

The College Achievement Alliance is made up of investigators and the faculty and staff of the campus who are committed to providing support for the investigators. The name "College Achievement Alliance" brings together the driving forces of poverty and middle class: the value of achievement and the value of relationships. That group works with the off-campus community through the local Bridges initiative. The community groups may already be providing support for GA graduates and working with various sectors as they adopt Bridges concepts.

College Achievement Alliance

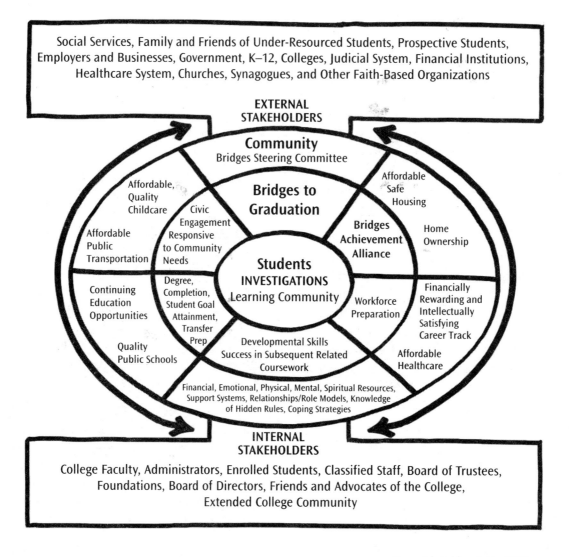

Source: Adapted from A. Liss, 2010.

Visit the Bridges website to learn more about what is happening in the postsecondary sector—or join the quarterly conference calls.

> 'Access without support is not opportunity.'
>
> —Vincent Tinto, Professor of Sociology, Syracuse (NY) University

Courts—Criminal Justice Sector

The Franklin County (Columbus, OH) Drug Court was the first drug court to offer Getting Ahead as an option for those who had established a program of recovery for themselves. Since then many problem-solving courts (drug, mental health, and family courts) have applied Bridges concepts and/or offered Getting Ahead. In Ohio there's a four-year, four-phase initiative to create pilot Bridges courts. Eighty court staff became Certified Bridges Trainers. Seven pilot courts are developing new policies and procedures that better serve people in poverty. Four of the courts sponsor or support GA workgroups and link graduates to Bridges Steering Committees in their communities.

Oklahoma has a statewide initiative to use Bridges in its reentry programs. The Office of Faith-based and Communities Initiatives is not only running that program but is coordinating the growth of Bridges in Oklahoma.

Getting Ahead is being offered to inmates at the Dixon Correctional Facility in Baton Rouge, LA; in Northeast Colorado; and in other jails and prisons. You can learn more about this by going to the Getting Ahead website.

Again, the point is that as courts and criminal justice entities apply Bridges and offer Getting Ahead, they build critical mass for the Bridges language, and they help change the environment for all people in poverty.

Health Sector

Some hospitals are using Bridges and Getting Ahead to improve retention rates of low-wage workers. Medical students in some medical schools are receiving Bridges training. A growing number of hospitals are using the concepts to improve patient care.

A large provider of training for state-tested nurse assistants (STNAs) in Ohio is using Getting Ahead with the students and plans to offer Bridges training to the hospitals and nursing homes that hire their students. In this way supervisors and nursing assistants will share a common language. Go to the Getting Ahead website to see results from Kent State University (OH) and Youngstown (OH) State University Getting Ahead workshops for nursing and other healthcare employees.

The community and sector applications change the paradigms and cultures of many organizations. In doing so, they broaden the bridge out of poverty for low-income people and those in poverty.

Some Lessons Learned by Institutions and Communities

1. Bridging social capital is such an important resource that it is part of every Bridges initiative. Bridges concepts enhance networking skills and strategies because they address class issues directly. Bringing people together across class lines is fraught with hidden problems unless everyone has the same basic understandings and language. All the models above are very intentional about building social capital.

2. GA graduates have often asked for Getting Ahead II. During Getting Ahead they realize that they need to know more about specific topics. A number of sites are offering one or more of these resource-building opportunities:

    a. Financial literacy classes

    b. GED classes

    c. Literacy

    d. Workforce development opportunities

    e. Emotional intelligence and anger management courses

    f. Parenting classes

    g. Assistance with Earned Income Tax Credit filings

3. Institutions and/or communities can help build mental/educational resources for GA grads within their own organization and with their partners by:

    a. Encouraging GA grads to prepare themselves for higher paying jobs within the organization by being trained on company time

b. Offering Investigations into Economic Class in America for college credit

   c. Urging job-training and placement partnerships to offer follow-up support during early employment and Bridges training to employers who hire GA grads

4. Institutions and/or communities have helped build financial resources by:

   a. Offering workforce development and placement

   b. Giving raises to low-wage employees upon completion of in-house, skill-building classes

   c. Working with banks to provide loans to entry-level employees and assuring repayment through paycheck withdrawals

   d. Providing a 50-cent raise to GA graduates upon completion of Getting Ahead

   e. Arranging to make GA graduates eligible for Habitat for Humanity homes

   f. Celebrating and honoring the employers who hire GA grads

Distinguishing Between Getting-By and Getting-Ahead Resources

We have learned that some resources *maintain* people in poverty, while some resources help people *make the transition out* of poverty. It's tempting to focus on the resources that help people build a new life, but it's not as simple as that. We need to understand the interplay between getting-by resources and getting-ahead resources.

Getting-by resources fall into three categories:

1. Maintenance at a basic level for an indefinite period, as in the case of Supplemental Security Income (SSI), Medicaid, and food stamps. This includes services for children, the aged, disabled, and blind who have limited income or resources.

2. Basic support for temporary resources, like unemployment, Temporary Assistance to Needy Families (TANF), energy assistance, Section 8 housing, childcare, and healthcare.

> 'Most families are so absorbed in their established patterns of daily tasks that they cannot focus on the larger world—and even at those moments when they are willing to, it is unclear what they can do.'
>
> —Daniel Taylor-Ide and Carl Taylor,
> *Just and Lasting Change: When Communities Own Their Futures*

3. Community organizations that are accessed by people in poverty: food pantries, soup kitchens, homeless shelters, domestic violence shelters, halfway houses, mental health and addiction centers, crisis lines, workforce development, and health departments.

The first two are government programs, the third is made up mostly of non-profit, non-governmental organizations.

Getting-by resources tend to be "needs based." GA investigators report that they go to these organizations to get their concrete needs met. Informal surveys of providers indicate that people in poverty go to 3–10 different organizations in the course of a year—with multiple visits to some. The experience goes something like this: People approach the organizations that can fulfill a need (food, housing, utilities, transportation, work, or counseling). Each organization gathers information, so the client tells his/her story again and again. Each organization determines need and eligibility and makes a plan with the client. The client leaves with things he/she needs to do based on the plan—and with some or all of the needs met. That means that the clients are carrying around 3–10 plans. The plans aren't coordinated, and sometimes they're contradictory. For example, an addictions treatment program may advise a client to not use mood-altering drugs, while a mental health clinic may in fact be prescribing mood-altering drugs to the client.

The needs-based model operates essentially in silos, each organization working on its own to get the outcomes it needs for its clients and to justify its own existence. Typically each of the organizations develops its own plans. This approach divides up clients' lives by the silos they enter and doesn't look at the whole person. It's a piecemeal approach.

Perhaps the biggest disincentives for people who begin the journey out of poverty are the "cliff" effects. These are the cutoff points for resources that are triggered by increases in income. For example, as someone moves up the income ladder from a minimum-wage job toward a self-sufficient wage, he/she will lose food stamps, WIC (Women, Infants and Children), housing assistance, and childcare support. In other words, the supports that provide stability are pulled out one by one before someone can even get to a self-sufficient wage. Stated differently, for every two steps forward individuals take to becoming self-sufficient, they're pulled one step back when they lose these supports.

The result of the needs-based model or the getting-by resources has not been to help people out of poverty but to label people in poverty as needy (because they keep coming back), deficient (because they're still in poverty), diseased (because poverty is a very stressful environment), and not to be trusted (because a relatively small percentage of them manipulate the system). To survive in poverty one must learn to navigate the systems and rules of various organizations. This is seen by some in the system as being dishonest.

In the needs-based approach, resources are "brought to" or made available to the client. The idea of building resources gets lost in the design of those programs and the delivery of those resources.

In a system like this it's no wonder that service providers become frustrated and jaded about clients whom they perceive in such a negative light. It's also easy to see why most people in poverty come to distrust the system.

Getting-ahead resources are different in that they are driven by power and intention. Rather than being a passive recipient of resources that are brought to you, you take charge of building resources. Getting Ahead is an example of a power-based model, sometimes referred to as an initiative-based or empowerment-based model. We choose to use the term power-based because over the years "initiative-based" became a loaded term, and "empowerment-based" suggests that someone with power is bestowing power to those who don't have it. In GA, investigators claim their power. The investigators do an analysis, make a plan, and begin to act as they pursue their future stories. Other examples of power-based approaches are Habitat for Humanity and the Family Independent Initiative based in Oakland, CA.

A great deal of success of the power-based model rests with the individuals who have to express their intention and act on it. It's ironic that many of the resources available in the needs-based model can be used by individuals who have an intention to build their resources. The likelihood of success would be improved if the organizations, communities, and funders adopted a getting-ahead approach to resources too.

Analyzing Getting-By vs. Getting-Ahead Resources

In Module 10 of the workbook, investigators are introduced to the chart used for assessing getting-by versus getting-ahead resources. They will use the chart to analyze their use of resources and changes they may need to make.

This chart can be used by sponsors and funders to determine how to balance the resources provided by an organization or community.

Analyzing the Difference Between Getting-By and Getting-Ahead Resources

	Getting-By Resources: 'Needs Based'	Getting-Ahead Resources: 'Power Based'
Financial		
Emotional		
Mental/Cognitive		
Language		
Social Capital		
Physical		
Spiritual		
Integrity and Trust		
Motivation and Persistence		
Relationships/Role Models		
Knowledge of Hidden Rules		

1. In your organization or community, what needs-based resources are available now to investigators?

2. In your organization or community, what power-based resources are available now to investigators?

3. If the resources can fit into both categories, determine where they go by answering this question: "How do the clients use the resources—for getting by or getting ahead?"

4. Are there any changes you need to make?

5. How can needs-based resources be turned into power-based resources?

Organizational issues: In these days of shrinking budgets, reduced staffs, and growing caseloads it's hard to deliver outcomes that justify further funding, unless of course we lower the bar and cut services. It's also hard to find money for staff development or time for building collaboratives. Yet it's through collaboration that your clients can benefit from the resource-building activities of other service providers. For example, in a community where there is a Bridges initiative, a drug court offender can be referred to a GA class in the community. On graduation the drug court participant is linked with other GA grads, is provided two middle-class mentors, and becomes eligible for a Habitat for Humanity house. Establishing a sober lifestyle by going through the drug court program is a benefit that raises the physical/emotional resources but, by adding the other benefits of a community model, more resources can be raised.

Funder frustrations: Donors, charities, United Ways, and foundations have expressed frustration with funding needs-based programming year after year. As good as the annual reports are, it seems as if the efforts simply maintain people in poverty.

Foundations have begun to take on Bridges as a communitywide initiative. They've been shifting some of their funding from needs-based to power-based. It's worth noting that resistance to power-based funding often comes from the agencies that provide needs-based programming. Those agencies are struggling to maintain their budgets and staff and are vested in the way they do business. For example, in a power-based model like Getting Ahead, the funding follows the people who are taking the initiative to build resources. The first instance of money going to investigators is when they're paid for their work in Getting Ahead. Budgeting $6,000 to $8,000 for Getting Ahead adds up quickly when communities run several groups. Taking those dollars out of the funding stream will certainly affect the needs-based organizations that were counting on them.

As the Bridges and Getting Ahead initiatives grow, there will be other times when GA graduates could benefit from financial support. It could take the form of a business start-up. One GA group is seeking funding to start a taxi business called Getting Ahead Cabs. It could be funding for the start-up of a Bridges Out of Poverty Student Union. The possibilities and opportunities are endless.

The chart on the previous page about getting-ahead and getting-by resources can be used to name the problem and to think through funding decisions.

NOTES

Support for Facilitators and Co-Facilitators

The importance of the facilitator's role can hardly be overstated. GA graduates rave about their facilitators at graduation celebrations and in interviews. They appreciate the facilitators for "never telling us what to do," for challenging the group, for being persistent in their questioning, and "… for keeping us on track."

Facilitators:

- Guide the learning process that is embedded in Getting Ahead
- Are an example of what it means to have relationships of mutual respect
- Demonstrate the principle that investigators are problem solvers and the experts regarding their own lives
- Practice tolerant impartiality, allowing the investigators and the group to work in a space that is free of judgments
- Demonstrate that investigators can be trusted to do what they need to do
- Help people get to where they want to go
- Listen, engage everyone, and encourage dialogue

Facilitators do not teach, lecture, use slideshows, stand before the class, or have all the answers.

Facilitator Knowledge, Skills, and Attitude

Here's the "short list" of necessary facilitator characteristics:

Knowledge

- A GA facilitator will be familiar with the concepts found in Getting Ahead while Getting Out
- A GA facilitator will be familiar with the Bridges Out of Poverty workshops as presented in community settings
- A GA facilitator will adhere to the approach to Getting Ahead presented in this User Guide

Skills

- Has ability to make connections with others, particularly people who or have been incarcerated and people living in poverty
- Can translate from the formal register to the casual register
- Can facilitate another person's self-discovery
- Can be empathetic without being "taken in"
- Has ability to work with a co-facilitator who was a previous workshop participant
- Has ability to work effectively even though from the dominant culture

Attitude

- Likes the investigators; in this work it's more important that we like the members of the workgroup than that they like us
- May be a returning citizen who doesn't carry the "baggage"
- Sees the best in someone who can't always see it in himself/herself
- Can laugh and have fun
- Is non-judgmental

Patterns in *Getting Out* Workbook

Recognizing the patterns in the *Getting Ahead while Getting Out* workbook will help the investigators move through the book more easily.

- **Headings and icons:** Instead of using the typical outline format, a reader can grasp the importance of each passage by the size of the font for the heading. Specific icons are used to identify activities, discussions, and planning activities. Each module begins with artwork, a brief statement about the content, and learning objectives. The modules end with a vocabulary list and a reading list.

- **Language:** The *Getting Out* workbook was written in the formal register at the seventh-grade reading level. The expectation is that investigators will take turns reading and that the facilitator and investigators will translate the information into the casual register as needed. Most of the learning will be done through the development of mental models that the investigators will help create and in group discussions. An investigator does not need to be fully literate in order to participate. Investigators will learn the vocabulary and terms needed to be effective in community settings.

- **The Triangle:** Referring to the Triangle (found in the workbook's Introduction) that has been taped to the wall, the facilitator can review the learning process with the investigators. Point out the element that is under investigation: understanding poverty, understanding "where I am," power, responsibility, or planning.

- **Learning objectives:** A "mediation" chart appears at the beginning of each module. It follows the pattern of mediation that identifies the stimulus (the *what*), assigns meaning (the *why*), and provides a strategy (the *how*). In Getting Ahead, it takes the form of "*what's* covered" (a mini table of contents for the module), "*why* it's important" (the *why*), and "*how* it's connected to you" (*how* it can be used). Doing this mediation with the investigators will help organize the information and open a gateway in the brain for learning—the "*why*-I-should-learn-this" gate.

- **New information and activities:** The pattern for investigating information has the following elements and headings: A new topic will be introduced, followed by one or more activities, and end with a discussion and, perhaps, a reflection.

- **Activities:** The most important activities are the mental models that investigators are asked to create. When the workbook is complete, each person should have a series of mental models that depict his/her life and plans. Some activities take the form of worksheets, such as the worksheet on calculating the debt-to-income ratio.

- **Discussion:** The discussion is led through a series of questions, which are designed to help investigators process the information. They're usually worded in such a way as to separate the problem from the person. It isn't necessary to ask and answer every question in the set.

- **Reflections:** In most of the modules, investigators are asked to think about how this information impacts them personally. It's OK to ask if anyone wants to share his/her insights with the group.

Knowledge of Oneself as a Facilitator

In Getting Ahead, investigators put at least 40 hours into studying their own lives and deciding what to do next. They attend 20 sessions, have hard conversations with fellow investigators, take time to reflect, and complete all the GA activities. GA investigators do a deep examination of their own lives.

Middle-class audiences are typically exposed to the same information in a 5½-hour Bridges workshop. But they usually don't have as much time to apply the information to themselves.

The two groups share a common language, but the GA graduates know the material intimately.

Facilitators who are from the dominant culture, the middle class, and who haven't done much examination of their own class experience may unconsciously "pull rank" on members of the group. Unconsciously because those who have normalized the dominant, middle-class ways of thinking, acting, and feeling aren't always aware of the power, status, and rank they have over others. It's hard to have relationships of mutual respect across the "great divide" of class.

Those who use the information in Bridges and Getting Ahead only to learn about poverty and reentry issues—and not themselves—can too easily maintain a distance from the object of their study, the "other."

Getting beyond this requires a good deal of work on the part of those from the stable environments to understand how they acquired their stability, resources, and status. And beyond that to know how they have benefited from societal structures that created such different economic environments.

Rankism is so deeply ingrained that even when people from the dominant culture move from being indifferent spectators to understanding the struggles of returning citizens and people in poverty and working with them, there is a tendency to become leaders of the transformation, to take charge.

Taking charge is "natural" for those who have rank. When working with people from different environments, it's a good idea to have a guide from that environment to point out ingrained prejudices and attitudes. It's a short step from seeing a problem to telling others what they should do. That is the definition of rankism: being able to tell someone what to do and expecting them to value (and follow!) the advice.

At the very core of this rankism is a lack of confidence and trust in the people's ability to think, to know, to act, and to build a new future story.

Experienced GA facilitators tell us that being in two-way relationships of learning with GA investigators and graduates is one of the great joys of facilitating Getting Ahead classes.

> 'I've worked for Head Start for over 14 years and, having facilitated the Getting Ahead group, I will never be the same. I know this is also true of the staff and families who have participated in Community Family Connections Groups.'
>
> –Stephanie Sutton, Licensed Professional Counselor and Program Coordinator, Heartland Programs, Salina, KS

Continuous Learning

When an individual gets started on the subjects of poverty, economic class, incarceration, and reentry, he/she will probably want to learn more about those topics. There are reading suggestions at the end of several modules in the *Getting Ahead* workbook.

The GA Learning Community, centered on the Getting Ahead website, includes conference calls, discussion pages, and an annual conference. There's literally "no end" to the innovations coming out of communities and organizations that use Bridges and Getting Ahead.

Things to Know: Michelle's Hidden Rules of Prison Life

While these rules apply primarily to inmates in correctional facilities, anyone entering a correctional facility for any reason should be aware of the following hidden rules of survival that inmates live by:

1. Mind your own business. Never ask another inmate why he/she is incarcerated.
2. Respect the space of another incarcerated person. Do not get within arm's length.
3. When there is a line in a correctional facility, especially a meal line, do not cut in.
4. Unless invited, do not go into a person's cell or bunk area. You could find yourself in an unwanted or dangerous situation.
5. If you are in someone's cell or bunk area, never sit on a person's bed. No one wants another person sitting on the place where they sleep. This is especially true in a female institution. Personal space is vital in a correctional facility. It may be all they have.
6. Do not ask for a favor from another inmate. If you do, remember the time will come when you will be expected to repay—double. This is called 2 for 1.
7. Many inmates run a store, a side hustle. That person will have anything you need, but remember there is a price for everything.
8. Beware if an inmate gives you something. Nothing is free in correctional facilities. This could be a sexual pass or grooming by a predator who will later expect to be repaid.
9. For your own safety, use common sense. Keep your mouth shut and your eyes open. Always be aware of your surroundings.
10. Never snitch. It can lead to serious harm.

Things Facilitators Need to Know About Working with Offenders

1. Abide by the rules and procedures of the institution.
2. It will take time for the inmates to open up to you and others in the group. Openness can be seen a sign of weakness, and the investigators may be unwilling at first to take the risk.
3. During the first class or two spend time talking with the inmates. Let them know why you are facilitating the classes. Tell them a little, but too much, about yourself. When they realize that you are a volunteer, without an agenda, you will start earning their trust, and the investigators will probably start opening up in class.
4. By making it clear to the inmates that this is their class, not yours, that they are the experts, not you, that you have no agenda, that you are not paid by the institution, the inmates will begin to realize that this program is different. All this will break down barriers between you the investigators.
5. Do not ask inmates personal questions, including why they are incarcerated. If they want you and others to know, they will tell you.
6. Avoid letting inmates do you any favors. They may expect something in return that you cannot provide.
7. Always be aware of your personal surroundings. While you may feel at ease in the institution and with the investigators, your safety must come first and foremost in all your actions.
8. As you develop trust with the investigators, be extremely mindful of the boundaries that must exist between the facilitators and the inmates.

9. Romantic relationships are forbidden by correctional institutions and by the Getting Ahead Model. Should that begin to occur the facilitator is required to withdraw from the program. Such occurrences can harm the program for everyone.

Things to Know About Working with Returning Citizens

1. Upon release it's likely that investigators will want to contact the facilitator, someone they know and trust. The 72-Hour Stability Plan should address this by having a team (including the facilitator) they can call.

2. Having team approaches for support are more effective than one-to-one mentoring approaches. Building bridging capital is the goal, but not over-reliance on one or two individuals.

3. Developing reentry programming is the work of the Bridges Collaboratives and/or reentry programs discussed in the Getting Out Reentry Model.

4. Returning citizens can be integrated into the support systems designed for people who attend Getting Ahead groups in the community.

5. While returning citizens tend to face more challenges than others, they need not carry the stigma of an "ex-offender." They can become part of the problem-solving team that makes up a Bridges Collaborative.

6. The Bridges Collaborative or reentry program should have a problem-solving approach, preferably based on the work of David Emerald, author of *The Power of TED*. This is an excellent resource for building emotional competence.

Things to Know About Working with Correctional Staff

1. Attend all classes required by the institution. The information, policies, and procedures are designed to assure the safety of everyone. Failure to comply with rules and procedures could jeopardize the Getting Out program in the facility.

2. It is not appropriate to challenge the rules. You should talk to staff about the rules if you don't understand the purpose of the rules.

3. Do not criticize any of the operations of the institution. Everything you say to staff and inmates will get back to the leadership and may cause you to lose the cooperation of the staff.

4. Learn which staff members support the goals of Getting Out. Some staff will not be supportive.

5. Have a contact person in the institution whom you can trust and who supports the program. Having someone to talk with will help resolve minor problems before they become serious.

6. Remember, you are entering their house. This is their business, and they are the experts in their institution. Respect that if you want *their* respect and cooperation.

7. There will be with certain staff you work with often. Do what you can to make their life easy; they are busy people with lots of responsibilities. A smile and a word of thanks go a long way toward building respect and cooperation.

8. Know what you are allowed to bring into the facility. This will probably be covered in the orientation and training for volunteers, but it's worth repeating because it's easy to lose the discipline of what constitutes contraband. This includes food, so check with your contact person about what can be brought in and for whom

Things to Know About Working with Adults

The theories and practices of Jane Vella, contained in her 2002 book *Learning to Listen, Learning to Teach,* are woven deeply into the fabric of Getting Ahead. Here are some (paraphrased) gems from that book that can keep the facilitator centered:

- The initial meeting between facilitator and investigator has to demonstrate the sense of inquiry and curiosity felt by the facilitator.
- The dialogue of learning is between two adults (i.e., facilitator and investigator or investigator and investigator).
- The immediacy perceived by investigators will affect their determination to continue working.
- Don't ever do what the investigator can do; don't ever decide what the investigator can decide.
- Motivation is magically enhanced when we learn about the themes of our own lives.
- Facilitators don't empower adult investigators; they encourage the use of the power that investigators were born with.
- Adults need reinforcement of the human equity between facilitator and investigator, as well as among investigators.

> *'It is more important for the [facilitators] to like their group members than for the group members to like them.'*
>
> –Richard Farson,
> *Management of the Absurd*

Information About Groups

Twenty sessions! Getting the *GA* workbook completed in 20 sessions will be a challenge. It's an intense learning experience that almost always makes a lasting impression. Here are some suggestions for getting through the material:

- Schedule three hours for the class so you can work for a full 2½ hours. Take a 10-minute break about halfway through the session.
- Monitor the percentage of time that is going into discussions. Overall, the time should be split about evenly between the content and discussion.
- Because the key concepts are sequenced, the facilitator doesn't have to "hit a home run" with every idea that's introduced. Ideas will be reinforced again and again.
- If the group members get onto a tangent, allow them some time to follow it through (within reason, of course). Some very interesting learning can take place when the group is following a thread.
- Assume people usually won't have read much of the text; most of the learning will take place in the group sessions. Use the text as a guide.
- Schedule make-up sessions with people who miss a session. It's important that each session begin with everyone at the same place in the content. The first time the *Getting Ahead while Getting Out* workbook is used, the facilitator will be responsible for announcing how and when make-up sessions will be handled; in later classes, the co-facilitator can schedule them.
- There are three times in the workbook where there are activities about time management and planning. These are part of a sequence leading up to the SMART Plan that will be done in Module 11. These are to be introduced and explained during the session but will be done on the investigator's time, not group time. Discuss the investigators' findings at the start of the next session. The following chart will give an idea of which modules to include in each session and when a time-management activity will take place.

Suggested Schedule of Modules per Session

SESSION	MODULE	TIME MANAGEMENT/PLANNING
Pre-GA Recruiting/Orientation	Overview and Orientation	
Session 1	Module 1: My Life upon Release	Time-Monitoring Sheets
Session 2	Module 1, continued	
Session 3	Module 2: Language	
Session 4	Module 2, continued	
Session 5	Module 3: Theory of Change	
Session 6	Module 3, continued	
Session 7	Module 4: Causes of Poverty	
Session 8	Module 4, continued	
Session 9	Module 4, continued Module 5: Hidden Rules	Time-Management Planning
Session 10	Module 5, continued	
Session 11	Module 6: Eleven Resources	Planning Backwards
Session 12	Module 6, continued	
Session 13	Module 7: Threat Assessment	
Session 14	Module 8: Self-Assessment	
Session 15	Module 8, continued Module 9: Community Assessment	
Session 16	Module 9, continued	
Session 17	Module 10: Building Resources	
Session 18	Module 10, continued	
Session 19	Module 11: Personal and Community Plans	72-Hour Stability Plan SMART Plan Resources Development Plan
Session 20	Module 11, continued	
Post-GA	Graduation Celebration	

Tips for Running the Group

Starting the Session

- Start each group by saying something like, "I'm glad you're here." It sounds simple, but it's significant.

- Rituals are important. Think of birthdays, weddings, funerals, graduations—and the opening and closing of each group. We don't prescribe rituals; we leave that to the creativity of the facilitator and the group.

- At the beginning of each session, establish a plan for the session by getting an agreement as to the agenda for the day; also discuss time frames.

- If you expect to run more than one group, you'll want to keep a log of each session in order to capture your impressions and lessons learned.

Encouraging Participation and Open Conversations

- Begin sessions with a question or activity that gets everyone to speak. This establishes that everyone is "present." It's like saying, "Hi, I'm here." This is an exception to any group rule that permits people to opt out of speaking.

- Break the group into sets of two or three people and have them discuss a point and report back to the group.

- Establish "left-handed conversations." "Right-handed conversations" is what we say. Left-handed is what we think. Sometimes we aren't really saying what we think. In Columbus, OH, Getting Ahead graduates met with doctors and medical students from The Ohio State University to talk about healthcare in poverty neighborhoods. There were two GA graduates at every table of 10 people. The groups conducted "left-handed conversations" in which the GA graduates played a big part. It was a safe, respectful, and deep conversation.

- Take turns reading, but allow the right to pass. If the investigators struggle with the content, break it down; read a short section (one or two paragraphs) and stop to talk about it.

- Some people don't contribute much, some may be coasting the whole way, and some may be cynical and challenging. Yet they are all contributing to the positive outcomes experienced by most of the investigators. They represent the cynics that everyone knows are in the community. So, overcoming the drag and challenges they represent is just a taste of the real world. The investigators know this too: "He's just like my Uncle Fred." In this way the man who is like Uncle Fred contributes too.

Creating Mental Models

- The GA investigators, not the facilitator, should do the actual work of labeling, lettering, and drawing.

  - The mental models need to be labeled accurately, starting with the title of the model. A rough draft of a model can always be redone so that it's more legible.

  - Models can usually be improved upon as understanding grows, so add to them over time.

  - Photos of the mental models created by the group can be used in newsletters, websites, and training.

- Mental models are used to help move back and forth between the concrete and the abstract. Some of the exercises in Getting Ahead start out seeming to be abstract; but, with an analogy, story, drawing, or exercise, they can be made concrete for the investigators.

  - For example, when learning about the Stages of Change, work an example (like going to college) as a group. On flipchart paper label the five Stages of Change, leaving plenty of room between each heading. Then give the investigators sticky-backed paper. Have them write phrases for what they would be thinking at each Stage of Change as they contemplated going to college. They can then attach their papers to the flipchart. This will illustrate the stages by engaging everyone and it will, without a doubt, provide a few laughs.

- When doing personal mental models, don't insist that investigators share their work with others. Do offer the opportunity, though, as one person's thinking often ignites the thinking of others.

- Mental models can be in many forms beyond those used in Getting Out. Be open to mental models using music, storytelling, poetry, plays, and even YouTube.

- Mental models that are created in Getting Ahead are so powerful that you and the sponsor may want to use some of them for publicity and educational purposes. Pictures truly are worth a thousand words. Some thoughts on this:

    1. Take pictures of all group mental models and, when the investigator is OK with it, any personal mental models. Group mental models are the property of the sponsor because the investigators were paid for them. Individual mental models belong to the investigator who created them, so you need permission to use any of them.

    2. Group mental models

        a. Label all mental models (for example, Mental Model of Poverty)

        b. Document on the back of each mental model the date it was created, group dates, location, facilitator's name, and contact information

    3. Individual mental models

        a. Label as above

        b. Get permission to use in publicity and/or education by your organization

        c. Get permission to for use by DeVol & Associates, LLC, and aha! Process, Inc.

        d. Get permission to use the owner's name in publicity (the GA investigator may allow you to use the personal mental model but not his/her name)

        e. Add information on the back as stated above

Commenting on the Work of Individuals and the Group

- Everyone likes praise, and very few of us like criticism, even when it's "constructive." When asked to comment on mental models by investigators, confine comments to the thinking that went into the model and the content of the model itself—without "giving it a grade." For example, when looking at someone's My Life upon Release Mental Model, say, "This drawing really shows how stressful your life is."

Praising or criticizing the work of an individual emphasizes the rank of the facilitator; it says that person is in a position to judge. Judging someone's work in any way ends up with him/her being accountable to the judge. We want investigators to be accountable to themselves and the group, not so much to the facilitator. The suggestion that the facilitator not judge the investigators doesn't extend to the investigators themselves. They are free to comment on each other's work as they please.

- Commenting on the work of the group as to "our hard work" and "our tight thinking" is fine. Statements like "We've done some good work here!" or "We need more detail here; how can we illustrate the point better?" recognize that the facilitator is also an investigator and equally responsible for the quality of the work.

- The facilitator needs to know that the individual's mental models are done. Seeing that they are done is different from evaluating or judging the content.

Questioning Techniques

- The discussion questions are designed to help process and develop the information presented in the *Getting Ahead while Getting Out* workbook and by the investigators. The questions are usually worded in such a way as to *separate the problem from the person* and avoid "leading" answers. A discussion might be started by asking an investigator to choose a question and respond to it. Encourage other investigators to add to the response—or pick up on other questions and instigate discussion. It isn't necessary to ask and answer every question.

- Questions can be roadblocks. When we ask a question we often telegraph our opinion of what a person should do, particularly when problem solving. For example, "Are you still with Bob?" is like saying, "You should dump Bob." This example is an exaggeration, but by paying attention to questioning techniques, one can see how often the "righting reflex" creeps into the question. The righting reflex is when you can see what the other person needs to do and you tell him/her so.

- Reflective listening is a technique that facilitators can use to encourage investigators to expand on their thinking. It doesn't require the use of questions. Reflective listening is done by repeating a phrase the speaker just used. This encourages the speaker to expand on the statement. Other questions using reflective listening can begin:

    ○ It sounds like …
    ○ It seems like …
    ○ So you think …
    ○ You feel …

  Remember that an interpretation is only a guess and may not match what was actually meant.

  Instead of asking questions, compare and contrast two statements to encourage the person to continue clarifying, for example: "You said earlier that you want to leave Bob, but now you're saying that you can't live without him."

- Encourage investigators to sharpen their thinking, use more precise language, and make the connections between ideas or between content and process. In the workbook this is called "tight thinking," and you can encourage it through recognition and feedback.

- Questions can be challenging, for example: "What do you want? What do you really want? How will you get there?"

Managing Problems

- Getting Ahead is not group therapy. This learning experience is not to resolve deep emotional issues. It is a cognitive approach that naturally evokes feelings. Notice that the discussion questions after each activity generally don't ask for feeling responses. This isn't to suppress feelings but to keep the work in the cognitive realm as much as possible. Typically, group members understand this need and, after the sessions, help those who struggle with their feelings. This is another reason to not hold more than two sessions a week. More than two sessions a week wouldn't give people enough time to digest the emotional aspects of the work.

  If an investigator does express feelings of hopelessness or thoughts of harming himself/herself or someone else, use the procedures of the sponsoring agency to get the person the help he/she needs. Also become familiar with community mental health services. Take the time to learn those procedures and have the information available for investigators. The facilitator's job, however, is to listen, question, support, and guide—not manage, tell, or solve.

- Highly disruptive individuals need to be removed from the group so others can engage in the learning process. This is difficult to do, but it helps if the group has made a group rule about disruptive behavior. Something like: "Those who insist on disrupting the learning of others have made a choice and will be asked to leave." With the group setting up such a rule, the enforcement of the rule doesn't fall so much on the facilitator as on the group. See it as positive peer pressure. How all this is done is at the discretion of the facilitator. It's important to leave the door open so the disruptive person can return to the group at another time.

- Be tuned in to the mood or underlying feeling in the room. Check with the group if the feeling is not "right." Masters of the casual register also are often masters of nonverbals. Masters of the formal register … not so much.

- Use 3x5 cards to find out what investigators are feeling, thinking, or needing. Have them turn in the cards to the facilitator to be addressed without naming names. This is a safe way to break through difficult moments (with disruptive members, for example).

- Every set of GA investigators is different, so every experience will be different. When you begin a new group don't expect or insist that a discovery made in an earlier group be made in the current group.

Managing Closure

At about the halfway point for the group, begin to periodically remind the investigators how many sessions are left. Make the reminders more frequent as the class nears conclusion. It's quite common for some of the group members to want to continue to meet more. Many have asked for "Getting Ahead II" or something called "Staying Ahead." Toward the latter phases of the investigations the group members will learn about the support systems that their home communities have in place. The investigators also should be encouraged to develop their own systems of support and/or to assist in designing and running the community programs.

Working with Co-Facilitators Who Were Former Investigators

One of the unique things about Getting Ahead is that former investigators are encouraged to become facilitators. That process usually begins with them first serving as a co-facilitator. Many GA graduates are now facilitating groups on their own. Like most facilitators, they attended online or onsite facilitator training events.

Training a co-facilitator assigns greater value to the process and provides evidence of the community's belief that investigators themselves are change leaders. The joint effort of facilitator and co-facilitator has many benefits—both real and symbolic—to all involved. Co-facilitators:

- Make the material more relevant
- Help bridge initial distrust or skepticism by investigators
- Build institutional capacity through the creation of experts within the community
- Create bridging social capital with the facilitator and the investigators
- Process the session with the facilitator and help improve the facilitator's performance
- Earn experience and respect by assisting the facilitator
- Model healthy behavior and investigation skills
- Assist in the translation from formal to casual register and vice versa
- Can follow up personally with investigators who miss a session

Building Relationships of Mutual Respect

Given that relationships are a driving force for most individuals from poverty, the facilitator is encouraged to be especially intentional about how and why he/she relates to the investigators. Relational learning doesn't mean the facilitator has to inquire about the investigator's offspring, spouse, parents, or pets—nor does it mean that the facilitator must provide services outside of class. But relational learning also doesn't preclude such actions.

What is very important is to be authentic, empathetic, respectful, and enthusiastic about the investigators' knowledge and learning. And what is most important is a willingness to network with investigators, to be bridging social capital for them within appropriate boundaries.

Following are some practical methods to achieve that sense of *support, insistence,* and *high expectations.* Sources are Clark Moustakas (1966), Stephen Brookfield (1990), Robert Marzano (2007), and Ruby Payne (2005, 2008).

Support

When investigating content, process, and mental models:

- Foster a sense of mutual respect through the co-investigative process
- Create a positive, constructive peer group to belong to by collaboratively establishing group rules for an emotionally and physically safe class environment
- Be explicit about how the course is organized; about the purpose of class activities, projects, and readings; and about the process at work
- Objectively present information for investigations; don't defend them or take a "side"
- Show concern; listen carefully to investigators and reinforce what motivates them
- Discover and acknowledge—inside or outside the workgroup—at least one interest, passion, skill, or talent for each investigator, especially if it relates to the Getting Ahead content
- Avoid showing favoritism toward an individual or group—or indicating bias or displeasure in relation to investigators who don't "perform" well

- Be aware that both intent and attitudes drive body language, and many investigators are skilled at reading nonverbal communication

Insistence

Regarding the motivation and persistence that come from the relationship, the facilitator is encouraged to:

- Be consistent in what you say and do—or investigators will have reason not to trust you
- Do what you say you will do; avoid breaking promises
- Coach only when asked
- Advocate for GA graduates
- Share aspects of yourself appropriately; explain what drew you to this workbook or how you became passionate about poverty issues
- Provide investigators access to GA graduates from previous groups and previously under-resourced individuals who attained success, yet maintained connectedness to their roots
- Hold the investigators accountable to themselves and to the group (which includes you)

High Expectations

Getting Ahead is demanding of the investigators; it isn't easy work. It's an adult learning experience that doesn't "lower the bar" or fatalistically accept lowered expectations. Getting Ahead is a safe place for investigators to take on challenges, to stretch themselves, and to learn and practice new skills.

Facilitators need to demonstrate the confidence they feel about the abilities of the investigators. If you find this to be true you can say, "I know you can, even when you don't think you can."

Support from Getting Ahead Network

When the GA group meets for the first time, the facilitator may well feel alone, afraid, and unprepared. And that's after reading this *User Guide* and attending an online or onsite training! There's nothing quite like the thrill of going into an experience where there's so little control.

But please know that there are many facilitators out there, ready to help you. The Getting Ahead Network is rather informal at this point, but it's very real and very big (getting bigger by the month). It could be that, in preparing to facilitate your group, you have already benefited from talking with someone from the Getting Ahead Network. It's my hope that you will join the Getting Ahead Network and that, before long, you find yourself helping another facilitator.

The Getting Ahead Network helps provide a:

- Learning community based on shared ideas
- Learning community made up of investigators, facilitators, sponsors, and community organizers
- Way to keep up with what is happening in different communities
- Way to solve problems
- Way to build bridging capital
- Way to deal with stress in informal settings
- Way to build resources
- Way to address poverty comprehensively
- Way to give back

How to network:

- Introduce yourself to someone new
- Attend meetings and conferences
- Give a business card, get a business card
- Ask if you can contact another GA facilitator you've met about issues that interest you both
- Find out how to connect by e-mail, phone, letters, Twitter, or Facebook
- Use the hidden rules of economic class
- Use language registers

Five Specific Benefits of GA Network

1. **The Getting Ahead website, like any other website, is constantly changing; it's never complete, never done.** Feeding it is like feeding a teenager who is always growing but never quite grows up. You can learn a lot by going to the website, the forum, and Facebook. These are just three places to become engaged in discussions.

   On the Getting Ahead website you will find a special section for the Getting Out Reentry Model. Please contribute to the collection of stories, reports, results, and best practices.

2. **The phone:** Watch for announcements about quarterly conference calls. Typically there are a guest speaker and a question-and-answer period.

3. **The conference:** Plan to attend the annual conference hosted by aha! Process, Inc. It's conducted every year in early October. Come with GA graduates; it's common for a team to attend the first year and provide a breakout session the second year.

4. **The preceptor:** When you've met a number of facilitators, consider asking someone to be your preceptor (tutor/mentor). A preceptor can be more help than a friend; the roles are very different. The preceptor can show you the ropes, troubleshoot, and process with you. Here are some things to think about with a preceptor:

    a. Define expectations for yourself and the preceptor

    b. Decide when and how often to meet or talk

    c. Decide on the length of the relationship

5. **Investigators:** Another unique thing about Getting Ahead is that you can learn so much from returning citizens. They are at the heart of the network.

You may want to review the unique features of GA content before launching into the modules. Here is a collection of Getting Ahead content's unique features.

4. Unique Features of Getting Ahead Content

UNIQUE FEATURES	BRIEF EXPLANATIONS
Getting Ahead uses the lens of economic class to address poverty.	There are other lenses as well that we recognize: race, ethnicity, age, gender, disability, and sexual identity. While we honor all lenses, our principal contribution to discussions on poverty is the lens of economic class.
Getting Ahead investigators create Mental Models of Economic Class and examine their lives in great depth.	Investigators are the source of much of the information in GA—information they use to analyze their own situations.
The Theory of Change that underlies GA is explained in detail.	The Theory of Change can free investigators from the tyranny of the moment and can put them in charge of their lives, even while they live in unstable conditions.
Getting Ahead addresses all four causes of poverty: the individual, community conditions, exploitation, and political/economic structures.	There are multiple causes of poverty that require a comprehensive approach to individual, institutional, and community solutions.
Getting Ahead defines poverty as "the extent to which an individual does without resources."	This definition gives us something concrete to do about poverty—build resources and assets.
Getting Ahead uses the hidden rules of class to help people understand each other better—and bring them together across class lines to solve community problems.	We raise class issues in order to help people establish relationships of mutual respect across class lines, in order to solve problems.
GA investigators do a self-assessment of their resources and an assessment of the community before building plans for both themselves and their communities.	GA investigators do a Threat Assessment regarding the first 72 hours after release from incarceration.
Getting Ahead isn't designed to bring about conformity or compliance. Rather, investigators deal critically and creatively with the reality of their lives and their communities.	We anticipate and prepare for the immediate challenges that returning citizens face upon their release.

Primary Principle: Seek Help from Getting Ahead Graduates

Faced with the challenge of figuring out what to do next to help GA grads, a surprising number of middle-class organizers have sought help from every quarter except the GA grads themselves. If you want to do relevant work, include GA grads in the conversation.

Dosage Counts

The more time spent on Getting Ahead and Bridges activities the better.

- Working on the next steps of the future story
- Attending classes, meetings
- Building resources
- The more time spent with people in the GA Network the better.
- Informal time: meeting for coffee, meals, films, parties, exercise, relaxing
- Formal time: interacting with people to work on poverty/ reentry/transition issues
- Connecting through newsletters, phone conversations, e-mail, Facebook, Twitter, and the Getting Ahead website forum

Finally ...

The next sections are module-by-module instructions and tips on how to do Getting Ahead while Getting Out. We have every confidence that you will have a wonderful experience. When you've caught your breath, please go to the website and tell us about your experience.

Best wishes!

> *'If you have come to help me, you can go home. But if you see my struggles as a part of your own survival, then perhaps we can work together.'*
>
> –Lila Watson, an Aboriginal Woman from Australia

NOTES

Module-by-Module Instructions

Before going into the instructions for each module, let's identify the patterns that will characterize the Getting Ahead while Getting Out experience. These patterns apply to every session, so they need to be described just once.

The Gathering Period

The best way to have a great group experience is to model what it takes to have one. Be accountable to the group by being there every time, being prepared, being on time, being there to greet them, and being there for them.

Share the ownership of the group with everyone in the group, so it's not just one or two people who help with the table and chairs, the coffee and food.

Decide on opening and closing rituals that provide structure, comfort, positive feelings, and a sense of belonging. Life is tough and to deal with it head-on the way we do in Getting Ahead, facilitators must show confidence in the investigators, trust in the curriculum, and consistency in attention to rituals.

The Drama of Prison Life

So much happens in an unstable environment that investigators may show up with their feelings already in turmoil. When people arrive for the workshop (and sometimes even in the middle of the session), general talking or side conversations will likely break out. Most of these conversations have to do with survival; they're about a recent crisis, a relationship, or the sharing of survival tips. So when you begin each session, take a few minutes for the group to unload or vent—and ask a volunteer to keep a running list of the issues that come up. This is crucial information on the problems and barriers that people face in high-stress, low-resource situations.

Once these issues are listed, you can move on more quickly the next time a given topic comes up. Anytime after the Theory of Change has been introduced (Module 3), these conversations can be described as conversations about the "concrete." The more time spent talking about being stuck in the concrete, the less time we have to talk about getting unstuck.

Some members of the group will probably use the participatory discourse pattern and circular story pattern. It's unlikely that many of these will be about the abstract information contained in the workbook. It would be a mistake to stop or correct this when it's really an opportunity to learn. Don't miss the chance to learn something that might help you or the group—some nuance of prison life, for example, or an illustration of how a hidden rule was broken.

Introducing New Information

New information is introduced throughout the *Getting Ahead while Getting Out* workbook. Here are some ways that you and the group can approach it:

- You can read the passages.

- Group members can take turns reading a paragraph each, allowing people to pass if they can't read, don't read well, or for whatever reason.

- For longer passages you can take turns reading, but stop after each paragraph or two to talk about what was covered and to clarify any unclear meanings.

- You can ask for a volunteer to prepare a way to present the information at the next session.

- You can use other readings from books, newspapers, or magazines—or play video clips to illustrate module material, provided you have the time. Video clips are a powerful way to learn, for instance, about the hidden rules of class. See Appendix H in the workbook for films and reading suggestions.

Since you'll be aware of the upcoming topics, you can have the investigators begin their work in advance. For example, there are investigations in Community Assessment (Module 9) that will take more time than most investigations, and they will need to be done outside of group time. This may be difficult in some correctional institutions.

Instructions

Charts like the upcoming one for Module 1 will provide instructions at a glance for facilitators.

Definitions of Section Headings

Agenda: This comes directly from the "What's Covered" section of the Learning Objectives in the *Getting Ahead while Getting Out* workbook.

Facilitator role: These are bare-bones instructions for the facilitator. When details are necessary, the chart will be "broken" and the additional information will be provided under the heading "Additional Information." This way, you don't have to look at the end of a long chart for the additional information. In the following example, the chart is broken to provide information about creating the Mental Model of Poverty. The chart then resumes to the end of the module.

The facilitator is also a co-investigator, as explained earlier, so role of the facilitator is to set up the learning experiences, then join the group in doing the work. The learning experience for facilitators who have not been incarcerated will be one they will never forget.

Investigator role: Under the principle of "Never do for adult learners what they can do for themselves," much of the investigators' role is simply to do the activity and to discuss it. That is where the work gets done. Don't underestimate the information and knowledge the investigators have.

Learning process: This describes the detailed process taking place within the module and reminds the facilitator of the larger underlying sequences that occur in Getting Ahead. For more about the five underlying sequences in Getting Ahead, see "Sequence and Reinforcement of Key Concepts Found in Getting Ahead" and "Getting Ahead—the Purpose of Each Module" in Appendixes 1 and 2.

Module 1
My Life upon Release

The first time the group meets, members will discover a unique feature of Getting Ahead is that no one will be "teaching" the class. They will learn that to be investigators they must be responsible for their own learning.

Before the workshop begins, re-create the Triangle found in the Introduction of the *Getting Ahead while Getting Out* workbook and tape it to the wall. It's best done in color so that the sections of the Triangle are distinct and easy to read. You will be using the Triangle to orient the investigators to the process as you move through the material.

Do introductions and develop the group rules. Tape the rules to the wall.

The investigators will learn that they are the experts on poverty, prison life, and what people need after their return to society to be successful. They will learn that their information is needed by community leaders to help lower the rate of recidivism.

The setting is safe, but the work is hard, even painful at times. What keeps investigators engaged is that virtually everything they talk about is relevant.

Agenda	Facilitator Role	Investigator Role	Learning Process
	Do introductions, group rules, and orient the group to the Triangle found in the Introduction to the *Getting Ahead while Getting Out* workbook.		This mental model, like all others done by the group, will be on the wall every session. It will help orient the investigators to the GA process.
Learn what a mental model is.	Define the role of an investigator and your role of co-investigator/facilitator. Explain the concept of mental models, or have the investigators take turns reading.		Set up the importance of mental models: developed together, along with shared experiences and knowledge.
Investigate what reentry will be like for returning citizens	Introduce the activity with questions provided in the workbook.	Take part in a discussion that leads right into doing the mental model.	The investigators are the experts; it may be their first learning experience where they are the experts, where they do most of the talking.
Make a Mental Model of My Life upon Release		Create the mental model.	This is a foundation for much of the learning to follow.
Create the Mental Model of Poverty	Provide directions and materials; make sure the mental model is labeled correctly.	Group work: Create the mental model.	

Additional Information on the My Life upon Release Mental Model

This is a perfect topic for the group's first investigation and discussion. Release is something that the investigators have all given thought to. As the group describes what life will be like, do not challenge ideas and plans that don't seem sound to you. Doing so would be pulling rank on the investigators and undermine the purpose of this session, which is to allow the group to do most of the talking. This is not the time to be building a successful and effective reentry plan. In fact, this is the way you learn their point of view. You can raise questions about stability, opportunities, hopes, relationships in order to help them take a deep look at the challenges they face.

This will be their first private mental model—something they don't have to share with anyone. It does form the beginning of a baseline, a platform they will use to push off from as they move toward a new future story.

Additional Information on the Mental Model of Poverty

The mental model below is an icon for the many and very different mental models that have been created. It is not meant to be an example to the group, but rather a visual representation for your benefit.

Mental Model of Poverty

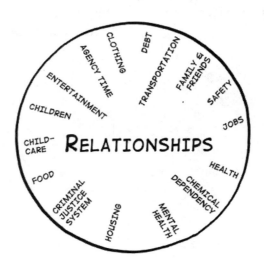

Concrete, Abstract

Powerless, Powerful

Unstable, Predictable

Tyranny of the moment, Long view

Math doesn't work, Financial security

Reactive problem solving, Proactive problem solving

Module 1: My Life upon Release

Notes (Tips) on the Mental Model of Poverty

1. Ask a group member to write MENTAL MODEL OF POVERTY at the top of some chart paper.

2. Assuming the group decides to capture the information about poverty in a circle or square, suggest that a space is left outside of the model so that short phrases can be added when the group shifts to analyzing the poverty experience.

3. The words that go inside the model describe the concrete experience of poverty, such as low wages, broken appliances, ER visits, etc. This can take a long time because people will probably tell stories and there is a lot to say. One group took almost two hours on this (which is unusually long) but they just weren't ready to stop until they had got it out. Don't rush this phase because it's important information.

4. When people criticize organizations in the community, do *not* defend them, even if you think you know better. If you do, you'll be pulling rank, and you'll be imposing the view of the dominant class.

> *We address relevant economic-class issues.*

5. When the information slows down, you can begin analyzing it. Start with the discussion questions, and when they begin seeing patterns and themes, ask them to write those terms around the outside of the circle. These don't all have to be done on this day. Add them as they come up naturally during upcoming investigations.

6. Listen to the conclusions that the group comes to, and suggest such analytical terms as problem-solvers, relationships (poverty is a relationship-based world), concrete, tyranny of the moment, unstable, powerless, and financial insecurity. At the very least, try to get the terms "Concrete" and "Tyranny of the moment" and "Relationships" on the mental model because in Module 3 those ideas will be used in the Theory of Change.

7. This mental model goes on the wall to the right of the group rules.

Agenda	Facilitator Role	Investigator Role	Learning Process
Make a Mental Model of Floor Plan of Apartment/ House Where I Will Live upon My Release.	Set up the activity, provide paper.	Individual work: Create a floor plan.	This is the segue between working on community issues and working on personal issues.
Investigate income and wage information.	Guide group through Housing Payment Threshold. Provide info on wages. Discuss percentage of income for housing. Provide info on the rules of money. These activities can be painful; be prepared to encourage them to see things through. Do calculations for themselves and assist other investigators who need help. Have discussions between each section.	Talking about housing naturally leads to thinking about payments and wages. Between each activity is more new information. Most of this investigation is about financial resources, but it is enough for people to begin thinking about their whole situation. Figure personal financial indicators. Introduce the debt-to-income (DTI) ratio activity following the discussion.	Talking about housing naturally leads to thinking about payments and wages. Between each activity is more new information. Most of this investigation is about financial resources, but it is enough for people to begin thinking about their whole situation. This may seem very abstract, yet it does represent one standard indicator.
Investigate "Where the Time Goes."	Set up the activity, pointing out that we will be creating plans at the end of Getting Ahead.	Do this activity between sessions.	There are two other activities about planning before we get to the big SMART Plan.
Closing	Remind the investigators about the vocabulary list. Suggest that investigators put into their Future Story Portfolio the My Life upon Release Mental Model and any other activities they wish.		

Experience tells us that Getting Ahead works because it starts with the investigators talking about what's important to them. When people are first released from incarceration, they usually live in poverty and go to many agencies to survive. They are used to be talked at and being told what to do. Here, in the first session, they experience the difference. It is challenging but it's real. The facilitator can help by reassuring group members that they can do it, that it will be worth it for them and for the others in the group.

Module 2

The Importance of Language

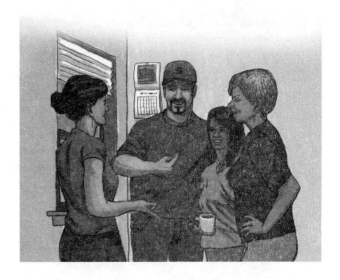

Investigators learn nine language concepts that can improve interactions with diverse groups of people by building respectful relationships, resolving conflicts, and exchanging information. Further, investigators can use the information to help prepare their children to learn and be more successful in school.

In this module there's a lot to read and absorb. The activities and discussions are crucial because they can break up the reading and keep the information relevant.

Agenda	Facilitator Role	Investigator Role	Learning Process
Learn about the registers of language and discourse patterns. Examine the role of prison talk.	First, the group will cover the foundational information on registers of language and discourse patterns. Remind investigators to keep a list of ideas they have and what they want to follow up on.	Participate in readings and discussions.	Investigating language is a safe topic that allows the group some time to build trust.
Learn about code switching between Standard American English and "neighborhood" language patterns.	Work through this information rather quickly. We are not learning how to code switch. We are simply learning that there's a positive way to address language differences between a neighborhood language and Standard American English.	Take part in the investigation and discussions.	This information is helpful to individuals in schools, colleges and correctional institutions. It gives teachers and instructors a nonjudgmental way to encourage the use of Standard American English in settings where it's necessary.
Examine the three "voices," as well as body language.	Cover the information on the voices with the investigators' help.	Participate in the investigation and discussions.	This is more information about language that puts into words common experiences and gives investigators options in the way they interact with family members and correctional officers and staff.

Additional Information About Language

Knowledge of language registers, discourse patterns, community languages, and the voices gives investigators both options and tools. These will be used in establishing/building relationships, resolving problems, and navigating unfamiliar settings such as incarceration and the return to the community from the institution.

The discussion questions in the *Getting Out* workbook are designed to draw out the learning through conversation rather than by having the facilitator direct-teach the information.

Place summary information about the nine language concepts, starting with registers and discourse patterns, on the wall. Also, place the mental models that are created by the group on the wall. This will make it easier for the group to return to and expand on the information in future workshops.

Though *Getting Ahead while Getting Out* is written for persons involved in the criminal justice system, most investigators have children, which is why we included this section in the book.

Language and Children

The following three sections are about language and children. In the interest of full disclosure, this is the one time in Getting Ahead when you will find an overt agenda! The individuals who were part of the pre-Getting Ahead investigations found value in this information and recommended that it stay in the workbook.

The agenda: A rich language experience in the first three years of life develops the brain and prepares children for school. Some investigators were thinking of their families and children when they chose to participate in Getting Ahead. It will be natural to learn this information for the sake of those children.

Remember, do not telegraph the agenda; let the investigators decide what they will take from this.

Agenda	Facilitator Role	Investigator Role	Learning Process
Explore the connection between story structures and a child's readiness for school.	Cover the information on story structure. Remind the group of the circular story pattern mentioned before. Have fun with the *Goldilocks* story.	Participate in the readings and discussion.	The transition to this topic is natural. We've talked about the circular story pattern and the "voices."
Investigate the importance of language experience in the first three years of life.	Work through the chart on the information that comes for the Hart/Risley study.	Discuss the meaning of the information.	This addresses how parents talk to their children and adds to the information that has already been covered. See notes below about the pain of learning this information.
Learn mediation strategies to help prepare children for school.	Introduce mediation and work the activity—the *what,* the *why,* and the *how.*	Participate in the activity and discussion.	This builds on previous sections (registers, discourse patterns, story structure, language experience, and mediation) that provide information parents can use.

Module 2: The Importance of Language

Additional Information About Mediation

Co-investigators and facilitators have reported that this information is often painful. It hurts to think that the way you've been raising your children may have been a significant factor in putting them at a learning disadvantage. If GA investigators don't verbalize their feelings, but you see nonverbals that suggest this, ask what group members are feeling.

Some people have been offended by the word "welfare" in the Hart/Risley study. You can explain that "welfare" was the term in use when the study was done, but it could be that most of the anger is really about the information in the study.

Being angry is OK, and it's OK to reject the information in the study. Once again you don't have to defend the study or the fact that it's part of Getting Ahead. Let group members work out their thoughts and feelings regarding this information.

If this topic interests you, consider reading:

- Hart, Betty, & Risley, Todd R. (1995). *Meaningful Differences in the Everyday Experience of Young American Children.* Baltimore, MD: Paul H. Brookes Publishing Co.

- Lareau, Annette. (2003). *Unequal Childhoods: Class, Race, and Family Life.* Berkeley, CA: University of California Press.

- Levine, Mel. (2002). *A Mind at a Time.* New York, NY: Simon & Schuster.

Language and Conflict

Agenda	Facilitator Role	Investigator Role	Learning Process
Use language to resolve conflicts.	Lead the investigation into the information on the Penance/Forgiveness Cycle.	Participate in the discussion.	The theme of families continues here. The example is of an adult child, but the dynamics would be similar with younger children. Styles of discipline segue nicely into the language of negotiation.
Learn the language of negotiation.	Co-investigate the material on "The Basics of Negotiating." Alert the investigators to the self-assessment they will be doing on their negotiating skills.	Take part in the investigation into negotiations.	Negotiation added to the other language skills can help investigators when they get to the planning and decision-making tables in the community.
Do a self-assessment of negotiation skills.		Complete the Self-Assessment of Negotiating Skills. Add this to the Future Story Portfolio.	While this is not an assessment of all the language issues raised in Getting Ahead, it does give the investigators more information about themselves that they can take into the planning phase.
Closing	Thank the group members and remind them of how many workgroup meetings are left.		

Additional Information on Negotiation

If you want to expand on the information about negotiations, there's an activity called the Ugli Orange Case in the *Investigations into Economic Class in America* workbook. In that activity, investigators work in pairs to negotiate a solution. It takes about 30 minutes.

Module 2: The Importance of Language

Module 3
Theory of Change

The information in this module can free people from the tyranny of the moment. This module is about metacognition, about GA investigators taking charge of their thinking.

Agenda	Facilitator Role	Investigator Role	Learning Process
Examine how we make changes.	Have group members talk about their My Life upon Release Mental Models and change.	Participate in the discussion.	We'll start with the topic of change itself.
Understand the "righting reflex."	Set up the exercise. Place the chart paper with the lists on the wall next to the Mental Model of Poverty.	Develop the list and work through the discussion questions.	This exercise starts with the concrete experience of going to agencies that want you to change.
Investigate how organizations try to get inmates, and other clients to change their behavior.	Co-investigate change, how hard it can be, and what GA investigators' experiences have been.	Participate in the discussion.	We're building a vocabulary about change with the goal of having GA investigators becoming experts on change.
Fill out the Stability Scale.	Set up the exercise.	Do the Stability Scale, and share findings in group discussion.	The Stability Scale can be a hard reality check. Allow the group time to process. The GA investigators might want to add this self-assessment tool to their Future Story Portfolio.
Learn the Theory of Change for Getting Ahead.	Draw a neat and colorful Theory of Change Mental Model. Place the mental model on the wall next to the Mental Model of Poverty. For more on the Theory of Change, read the text beginning on p. 85.	Copy the Theory of Change as the facilitator draws it. Add it to your Future Story Portfolio.	This is the only mental model that the facilitator will create. Don't expect everyone to "get" the mental model when you do it. Don't worry; you will be reinforcing the theory. See Appendix 1 for "Sequence and Reinforcement of Key Concepts Found in Getting Ahead."

Additional Information About the Process of Change Mental Model

Concept

The Mental Model of the Process of Change will be useful in two ways. First, it will help GA investigators realize what happens in this workbook: People move from the concrete (the tyranny of the moment) to the abstract and a new future story. Second, it will help manage the group discussions, which can very easily get stuck in storytelling.

Instructions

Even though the Theory of Change Mental Model is in each investigator's workbook, it helps if you draw the mental model as you describe the Theory of Change. You also will want to save this drawing in the group's collection of mental models that are hung on the walls.

This mental model will help you and the group *think* about the progress being made. You will likely find that the GA investigators have a lot to talk about because so many things can go wrong in the course of a week. The mental model can be used to show how, if we stay fixated on the problems of today, we will have a very hard time getting to the new information. It's a way the GA investigators can monitor themselves and keep moving through the material. If the group gets stuck in storytelling, refer to the mental model and ask:

- *Are we getting to the new information?*
- *Are we able to let go of the concrete problems of today enough so we can work on the abstract content of today's investigation?*

You will find that the group members will begin to limit the time they spend on the concrete in order to get to the abstract. Be alert to how GA investigators shift from the concrete to the abstract and comment on it. GA investigators have said things like: "OK, we've got to stop talking about these problems, or we'll never get to the new stuff."

Investigators will be learning metacognition—how to *think about one's thinking*. The first time this might have happened was when the group investigated the percentage of income spent on housing—and began to summarize findings about the Mental Model of Poverty. Some members of the group might have changed the way they thought about poverty and near poverty; in other words, they changed their own mental model. That is working in the abstract. Recognize and encourage it.

> *'The need to act overwhelms any willingness people have to learn.'*
>
> –Peter Schwartz,
> *The Art of the Long View*

The Theory of Change Mental Model is a foundational piece of the process in the GA workbook. The vocabulary being developed provides a shared understanding of this new material. This will allow the group members to proceed in developing a framework of ideas to apply within their individual and community plans.

The activities in Module 1 created cognitive dissonance, a discrepancy in the minds of GA investigators between what is and what could be. Future modules will provide an opportunity to resolve the dissonance, but for a time most of the GA investigators may be in an uncomfortable space. And that's OK. The Theory of Change Mental Model cannot be developed without having first done the My Life upon Release Mental Model. The Theory of Change is reinforced in Modules 6, 9, and 10, as well as in Module 11's planning activities. So it's all right if some GA investigators don't fully grasp the process of change the first time it's discussed. The GA investigators will eventually teach each other this concept. One of the benefits of sequencing in this way is that the facilitator doesn't have to knock the ball out of the park with every concept the first time it's introduced.

Here's a step-by-step procedure for developing this mental model:

1. Draw the inner circle and label it "My Life upon Release." This represents the mental model that each person drew of his/her own situation. Next, label this as "Concrete," meaning it requires people to solve immediate problems all day long and doesn't give them much opportunity to take on abstract issues. Explain that this is where we often get stuck. This is the tyranny of the moment. People in persistent poverty, victims of natural disasters, and civilian populations in war, for example, have to solve concrete problems with concrete solutions over and over, finding a way to survive, to get by, to solve the same problems again and again. (This discussion reinforces the learning from Module 1 that you already completed.)

Draw the outer circle and label it "Abstract." Define abstract as:

Detachment	....	Being able to separate yourself from your problem, as in: "*Poverty* is the problem. *I* am not the problem."
Objectivity	....	Stepping away from the Mental Model of My Life upon Release and studying the mental model honestly and fairly.
New information	....	This comes from doing investigations, not settling for the obvious answers.
New ideas	....	You have new insights, "aha" moments, different solutions to your situation.
Analysis	....	This is when you can compare and contrast, break the information down into smaller parts, or look at the big picture.
Thinking	....	This is when you reflect about what you are seeing and learning.
Education	....	You choose to learn more about topics that you find interesting or important.
Plans	....	You shape new information and new ideas into concrete action steps.
Support	....	Looking ahead, you know that you'll need a team to help you and encourage you.

To get out of the tyranny of the moment and to change our lives, we must be able to get to the abstract.

2. Draw the set of rectangles (representing plans) and the three lines (representing procedural steps), making the point that when resources are low, people need concrete solutions. Label this "Concrete Plans." Guide a discussion about how immediate concrete solutions often aren't effective long-range solutions. You might start the discussion with, "When the electricity has been cut off, we aren't interested in budgeting information as much as we're interested in getting the heat and lights back on." We have to get into the abstract to really solve our problems by detaching—and by using new information to develop new ideas or solutions.

3. Describe how unstable, under-resourced environments require that people use reactive skills to get concrete solutions to concrete problems. Draw an arrow from the word "Concrete" in the center of the model to the word "Concrete," which is beside the symbol for planning, to illustrate how people go to agencies and friends to get those concrete needs met. Point out that there isn't time for the abstract when one is in crisis mode. Now draw a line from the word "Concrete" in the center to the word "Abstract" to illustrate how a person can choose to think in the abstract even during a crisis. Then draw a line from "Abstract" to the word "Concrete" beside the plan. This illustrates that a plan including *new information* will produce a solution that can lead to a completely *new direction* in life. When bogged down in the tyranny of the moment, people are forced to solve the same problem in the same way over and over. *The Theory of Change, on the other hand, is the key to increasing economic stability.*

4. Now add the abstract concepts presented in Getting Ahead: economic realities (the Mental Model of Poverty and the research on the causes of poverty), the Stages of Change so we can track our own success, and Payne's information (resources and hidden rules of class). This is the same information that is in the Triangle, an *abstract* representation of what happens during Getting Ahead.

5. Write the word "PLANS" into the set of rectangles and "Procedural Steps" for the three lines below. This is where we begin to emphasize the value of planning and lists, which will be explored in greater detail in Module 4.

6. Now talk about how people move from the inner circle to the outer circle, how they cross that thin line.

In other words, how do we, when we are in "crisis mode," find a way to detach so we can think abstractly? The GA investigators' workbook already has offered three ways this can be done:

   a. By creating mental models: As we learned in Module 1, mental models can help us see the big picture, connections, relationships, and options—all without a lot of words.

   b. By developing social capital: The second way is to have people (like the facilitator and the other GA investigators) who can make the information relevant and meaningful.

   c. By using "mediation": Here we investigate the *what* (past and present); the *why* (new information, including the disparity between what is and what could be); and the *how* (envisioning a new future story and developing a plan to get there).

> 'The "concrete" circle in the Theory of Change Mental Model is like a ball in the pit of your stomach—you don't know whether to throw up or what ...'
>
> –Getting Ahead Investigator, Bucks County, PA

Mental Model of Getting Ahead
Theory of Change

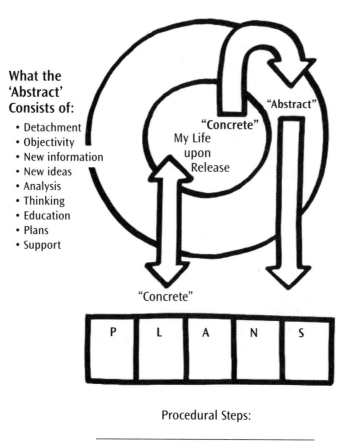

What the 'Abstract' Consists of:
- Detachment
- Objectivity
- New information
- New ideas
- Analysis
- Thinking
- Education
- Plans
- Support

The content of the *Getting Out* workbook found in Modules 2–6 is the new information that investigators will use to develop their plans and support system.

Procedural Steps:

_____
_____
_____

> 'I usually couldn't concentrate when our sessions began because I was too caught up in all of my problems. I also wondered how is it possible to learn anything when no one is telling us what to do? Yet every Tuesday someone comments, "Isn't it amazing how much we learned?!"'
>
> —Bernard, Getting Ahead Graduate, Billings, MT

Agenda	Facilitator Role	Investigator Role	Learning Process
Learn the Stages of Change	Lead the group through the information on the Stages of Change that includes the example of a smoker. Have the group work through the steps together, choosing another example that is relevant to someone recently released from incarceration.	Work as a group to illustrate how the Stages of Change work for a topic different from the example of a smoker.	This information allows GA investigators to name and monitor their own Stage of Change.
Closing	Have the group look at the vocabulary list and add other words they have identified.		

The information on the Stages of Change will come up again when discussing motivation in Module 6 and more frequently as we work the development of a plan in Module 10. The goal is to help GA investigators gain power in their lives by taking charge of and monitoring their own changes.

It's important for GA investigators to know that the Stages of Change almost never occur in a straight line and that relapse is normal. The point is that when there's a relapse we don't have to start all over but can go back to the preparation or action stage.

> *'Change comes before we see it; the tree knows before we see the change in colors.'*
>
> –Clara Ross, South Bend, IN

Experience tells us that this information becomes more significant over the long haul after graduating from Getting Ahead. Change isn't easy. Often the changes get stalled because of community or systemic barriers. Sometimes the changes that get put in motion begin taking a toll on relationships. Sometimes the changes that have taken place challenge one's own sense of identity. Knowledge of the Stages of Change is of some help during transition, but needs to be bolstered by building lots of social capital, all topics in upcoming modules.

Additional activity: Introduced here, Maslow's Hierarchy of Needs can give investigators another way to look at themselves. See Appendix 6 for a mental model you can share with the group. The group can refer back to this when doing the self-assessment. Note that the bottom half of Maslow's hierarchy is about getting-by resources, while the top half is about getting-ahead resources.

The My Life upon Release Mental Model conceptualizes the discrepancy between what life is like now and what life could be. This discrepancy creates the cognitive dissonance that is the foundational catalyst for change. Stated differently, the difference between "what is" and "what could be" fuels the motivation needed to actualize personal growth. Getting Ahead then provides invitations and opportunities that put GA investigators in charge of their own learning and planning.

NOTES

Module 4

The Rich/Poor Gap and Research on Causes of Poverty

This module is one of the most demanding for facilitators. Investigate it along with the group and trust that the learning process will provide the investigators with several ways of looking at their own situations. Help the investigators by asking them, "How does this apply to you?" They will be doing the work of learning and connecting the dots.

On the surface this information seems far removed from the people who are incarcerated and those struggling just to keep their heads above water. Admittedly, much of the information is rather abstract. It is our job as facilitators, however, to make the information as relevant as possible to the situations of the investigators.

These topics are very much in the public mind at the time of this writing and are likely to remain so for many years to come. Both conservatives and liberals/progressives have staked out their positions on the causes of and solutions to poverty. As you'll see in the Research Continuum, they both tend to take an either/or stance: conservatives at the "individual" end of the continuum, liberals at the "systemic" end. It's as if they truly think that poverty is caused only by the individual or the system. The Getting Ahead stance is that poverty is caused both by the choices of individuals in poverty and by systemic conditions ... and everything in between. One unique thing that GA offers is a straightforward both/and approach that conservatives and liberals can and do embrace. Getting Ahead is being used by people, institutions, and communities from all points on the political spectrum.

Whatever your personal political persuasion, as a facilitator you're expected to present this information without imposing your agenda on your co-investigators. It's important to note that Getting Ahead itself is focused largely on individual action. It's also important that Getting Ahead sites address the other causes of poverty and mass incarceration: community conditions, predators/exploitation, and political/economic structures. Without those added factors, the blame for poverty in our communities would fall almost entirely on the investigators themselves.

What we have learned from the many Bridges and Getting Ahead sites is this: People in poverty and returning citizens need to change—but no more than anyone else in our communities.

Key Points About Module 4

1. Our main purpose in exploring the causes of poverty and incarceration is to illustrate that poverty and incarceration is about more than the choices of the individual. There are many things that contribute to poverty and incarceration over which individuals have no control whatsoever. Of course, it would be better if investigators come to this conclusion themselves, rather than having the facilitators "teach" it. Another reason to investigate this information is to give people ways to analyze policies and programs set forth by legislators and others in positions of power. Investigators will usually be able to tell rather quickly if the proposed policies and programs are comprehensive—or if they fixate on one particular cause of poverty or incarceration.

2. Module 4 also can give investigators insight into the mindsets of people they encounter. They'll be able to tell who thinks that poverty and mass incarceration is the result of bad choices made by individuals, who thinks it's the result of political/economic structures, and who thinks it's a combination of all the causes. Getting Ahead graduates tell us that most of the time they can determine someone's political persuasion within minutes.

3. Encourage investigators to analyze the strategies that arise out of the research topics. An obvious example would be the research on single parenthood and the strategy of marriage promotion that is offered as a solution. Policy proposals can be decoded by using the continuum to determine how comprehensive they are in their approach to poverty and lowering the rate of recidivism. Another unique feature of Getting Ahead is that it proposes that all causes of poverty and incarceration be addressed.

4. To become comfortable leading an investigation into this information, you will want to read at least one suggested source for each category of research. You'll find it easier to talk about the causes of poverty and incarceration if you have one solid example for each area of research. See the reading list for this module in the *Getting Ahead while Getting Out* workbook.

Agenda	Facilitator Role	Investigator Role	Learning Process
Understand the range of causes of poverty and incarceration—from personal to systemic.	The first activity is a quick way to make the coming information relevant. Review the elements of the Research Continuum, headings, definitions, and topics.	Apply the information to themselves and their communities.	With the first exercise, start with anchoring the information in the experience and knowledge of the group. This module deepens as it goes, ending with a Personal Chart on Economic Class and a writing assignment: "My Economic Class Story."

Additional Information About Causes of Poverty and Incarceration

As investigators begin to articulate insights they have had, suggest they create a list of the new ideas. There is so much information in this module that it would be easy to lose sight of the new learning.

As investigators express their opinions—some of them political, some of them critical—remain detached and non-judgmental. If arguments should arise, ask the group to remember the *both/and* feature that honors the viewpoints of both conservatives and progressives.

Individual Behaviors and Circumstances

The text on individual choices and behaviors is the shortest because it is the one that investigators know the most about already. This is not the time to delve into the research on individual choice; in later modules the investigators will be doing in-depth analysis of their own resources and choices.

Community Conditions

This is a brief look at the conditions in the local community. In Module 9 the investigators will be doing a community assessment, so think of these questions as an introduction to Module 9.

You might run down the list of topics in the Community Conditions column of the Causes of Poverty and Incarceration—Research Continuum chart in Module 4 of the *Getting Ahead while Getting Out* workbook to find out what the investigators think of the items.

Exploitation

Agenda	Facilitator Role	Investigator Role	Learning Process
Establish a strategy to protect yourself from predators.	Set up an investigation into predatory businesses. Do not do this work *for* the investigators. Remind the investigators to make notes of new information that is meaningful to them.	Investigate how you and your family, friends, and neighbors have used legal and illegal predatory businesses.	Two things are going on here: 1) The group is learning who the predators are. 2) This is an opportunity to illustrate how the Theory of Change works in real situations (see following example regarding predators).

Additional Information About Predators

Illustrate the Theory of Change by examining the typical practices of a predator.

- Predators provide a concrete and immediate solution to a specific problem. When your paycheck doesn't cover the entire week and you need cash, the payday lender is there for you.

- Predators provide a comfortable environment and an easy shopping experience. Parking is convenient, and there's no bullet-proof glass between you and the cashier. The paperwork doesn't take long. You feel respected.

- Predators know that most people will not read the fine print. And even if they did, where else would they go? The predator is usually the last resort, and you feel relieved that the loan will take care of the immediate problem.

- Predators know you'll be back. They know that you're living in a situation that isn't going to change easily. You will almost certainly need their services again.

So in summary, predators know that the victim is in the tyranny of the moment, that he/she needs an immediate concrete solution. They keep the paperwork to a minimum and are not intrusive (the way many social services agencies are), which feels respectful. As one person put it, "I thought the guy at the lease/purchase place was my friend." They literally *bank* on the fact that the victim won't go to the abstract and figure out what the true cost and consequences are. By using the Getting Ahead Theory of Change, the victim can overcome the tyranny of the moment by instead going to the abstract; reading the fine print; and looking for better, longer term solutions.

What are all the costs of going to the predator?

What are all the costs of going to an alternative provider?

Agenda	Facilitator Role	Investigator Role	Learning Process
Learn how the middle class was created.	Read or have the group read the section titled "Creation of the Middle Class." Stop after each paragraph or two and discuss how the information relates to the investigators. Review the "Household Median Net Worth by Race, 2009" information.	Participate in the reading and discussion.	This is more hard information to examine, especially for those who have not acquired many assets. The information about the middle class includes information about race. This information will help the investigators when they are doing the Personal Chart on Economic Class and "My Economic Class Story."
Learn about disparity in income and wealth.	Use the following United for a Fair Economy (UFE) exercises (through p. 101); it isn't necessary to do every activity. Direct the group to Appendix C in the workbook to learn about taxes in a section titled "Who Pays the Most Taxes? What Does It Mean to the Community?" Remind the investigators to make notes about new information that is significant to them.	Participate in the creation of the mental models that use volunteers to illustrate the information with their bodies.	The UFE activities are fun to do; they get the group members out of their chairs and outdoors or in a hallway or gym. Groups react differently to this information and often have strong feelings about it. Again, there is no need for you to critique their points of view.

Political/Economic Structures

Income Quintiles Activity

This activity compares income distribution in two recent periods of economic growth in the U.S. To demonstrate the growth and/or decline of incomes over time, five volunteer participants are asked to come up and stand in the front of the room. [For this activity to work well, the volunteers will need plenty of space to move forward and some space to move back.] It is important that the facilitator focus the group's attention on the top one to 5% of the population—the greatest beneficiaries of the growing divide. It is also important that everyone gets a chance to see where they fit, in terms of income distribution.

Most folks think they are "middle income," and it is often a revelation to learn otherwise. We demonstrate the 1979–2009 time period before the 1947–79 period because our experience has shown the activity to be more memorable that way. It also gets folks thinking about public programs that generally supported greater economic equality in the 1950s and 1960s (e.g., the GI Bill, appropriations for higher education, housing, and infrastructure projects, more favorable law enforcement, etc.).

Props

It is helpful to have 8½×11 placards for each volunteer participant to hold, identifying the quintiles and showing the income ranges.

Instructions

1. We are going to look at the changes in family income during two recent periods of economic growth. First, let's talk a little about income. What are some examples of income? (wages, salary, savings account interest, Social Security check, rent from owning real estate, capital gains from selling investments, dividends from stocks, gifts, etc.). Now let's have five volunteers come to the front of the room. Please stand should to shoulder. [The facilitator hands each volunteer a placard showing the income range—in pre-tax, year 2009 dollars—of the quintile they represent.]

2. Listen to this introduction to the concept of income quintiles. Economists often talk about the U.S. population in "quintiles" or "fifths" of the population. They imagine the entire population of the U.S. lined up in order, from the lowest income to the highest. They then divide that line into five equal parts. This activity looks at what happened to the incomes during two periods of economic growth: 1947–79 and 1979–2009. Let's look at some of the folks who are in these quintiles. What sorts of occupations or economic situations would you imagine fall into each quintile? Remember, this is family income. (A family is two or more related individuals living together.)

3. The following demonstration may seem like the childhood game "Mother May I" (also known as "Giant Steps"). Each volunteer, representing a quintile or fifth (20%) of the U.S. population, will step forward or back according to whether their income gained or declined. Each step equals a 5% change, so, for example, two steps forward would indicate an income gain of 10%.

4. Between 1979 and 2009 (top chart on p. 90 of *Getting Out* workbook), here's what happened:

Quintile	Steps	Percentage Change	Yearly Income Range (2009) (family income before tax)
Lowest	1½ steps backward	−7%	$0–26,934
Second	1 step forward	+4%	$26,934–47,914
Middle	2 steps forward	+11%	$47,914–73,338
Fourth	4½ steps forward	+23%	$73,338–112,540
Highest	10 steps forward	+49%	$112,540 and higher

5. Watch what happens when we break that top quintile down even further and look first at the richest 5% of the population. Rather than tear off the arm of our highest quintile volunteer, let's have another volunteer from the audience represent the top 5%—people with incomes of $200,000 and up. From 1979 to 2009, the income of this group grew 73%! [From the spot where the top quintile is standing, the sixth volunteer takes 5½ additional steps forward—15½ steps in total from the starting line.]

And if we break down the top quintile even further and look at just the top 1%, we see exactly where the greatest income growth went. This small group gained 169%, just about 34 steps from the starting line. And the calculation for the top 1% does not include income from capital gains.

Quintile	Steps	Percentage Change	Yearly Income Range (2009) (family income before tax)
Top 5%	15½ steps forward	+73%	$200,000 and up
Top 1%	34 steps forward	+169%	$1.2 million and up

6. Watch this demonstration of what happened to the quintiles during the post-war years: 1947–79. We will start with the top four quintiles. This time (for space reasons), for every 10% gain, the volunteer will take a step forward. How well (number of steps forward or back) do you think the bottom quintile fared? How about the top 5%? What strikes you about these two periods in history?

Quintile	Steps	Percentage Change
Lowest	12 steps forward	+116%
Second	10 steps forward	+100%
Middle	11 steps forward	+111%
Fourth	11½ steps forward	+114%
Highest	10 steps forward	+99%
Top 5%	8½ steps forward	+86%

7. What conclusions do you draw about family incomes? What questions do you have?

8. Please review the upper chart on p. 90 ("Real Family Income Growth from 1979 to 2009") and the lower chart on p. 90 ("Real Family Income Growth from 1947 to 1979"). What are your questions?

Source: Adapted from *The Growing Divide: Inequality and the Roots of Economic Insecurity Trainer's Manual,* 2009.

 The CEO Pay Gap Activity

Facilitator's Goals

a. Dramatize the widening gap between the highest- and the average-paid workers in the U.S.

b. Explore why the wage gap in the U.S. is wider than in other nations. This activity is a "human graph" that illustrates the ratio between those who are paid the most—chief executive officers (CEOs) and average workers. Six volunteers, each carrying an identifying sign, will role play CEOs and average workers from three different countries. The volunteers representing CEOs will move across the room in proportion to the difference between their compensation and their workers' pay.

Props for this learning activity

Placards that say:

"Japanese Average Worker"   "German Average Worker"   "U.S. Average Worker"
"Japanese CEO"   "German CEO"   "U.S. CEO"

Instructions

1. Let's have six volunteers who will represent workers or CEOs from the U.S., Japan, and Germany line up in two columns facing the audience. One column represents the CEOs and the other column are average workers.* Please hold a sign identifying who you are so all can see.

   The U.S., Japanese, and German CEOs will move sideways step by step with each step equal to a five times ratio (therefore, if an average worker was paid $20,000 and the highest paid executive receives ten times that amount—$200,000—then they would be two steps apart).

   The income ratio between the German CEO and the German worker is about 21 to 1. The German CEO takes four sideways steps. Next, the Japanese CEO—a little less than the German CEO (9 to 1): two sideways steps. In the U.S. the ratio is 44 to 1: nine steps. (See chart on p. 92 of the workbook.)

   * These comparisons are for industrial corporations with sales of approximately $500 million, surveyed by *BusinessWeek* magazine in 2009.

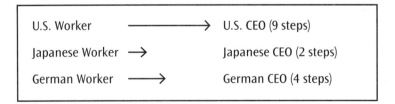

2. Now, if we look at the 365 largest U.S. firms as reported in the Annual Executive Pay report by *BusinessWeek*, in 1980 the ratio of CEO pay to the average worker was 42 to 1 (eight steps apart). In 2004 the ratio was 431 to 1 (86 steps apart).

3. What strikes you about the income ratio comparison? How would you explain the difference in income ratio between the U.S. and Germany and Japan? On p. 91 of the workbook, you might also check out a 48-year analysis of CEO pay versus the pay of average U.S. workers.

Talking Points

- CEO over-compensation hurts average Americans. It transfers wealth upward from employees and shareholders to already affluent top executives.

- Organizational management guru Peter Drucker believes that corporations should flatten out their structures—which exist primarily to justify excessive salary differentials. He speaks specifically of establishing a wage ratio between top and bottom.

- In recent years, shareholder activists have sparked public attention to the issue of the huge gap between CEO and worker pay. More than 350 resolutions on executive compensation were filed in 2007. Whole Foods Market set a positive example by limiting CEO John Mackey's salary to no more than 14 times the pay of the average frontline employee. Contact UFE for more information about shareholder campaigns for pay equity.

- Angelo Mozilo, CEO of Countrywide Financial, a firm at the heart of the sub-prime mortgage fiasco, earned $102.8 million in 2008. That means he made $1,976,923 a week; $282,418 a day; $35,302 an hour. He earned 90 times the minimum hourly wage every minute! His compensation is about equivalent to 3,000 well-paid account managers. Because of the cap on wages that are subject to the Social Security tax, Mozilo was done paying into Social Security at 1 p.m. on January 2, before the end of his first day of work, while most of us saw money taken out of every one of our paychecks.

Top Ten CEOs in 2008
(total compensation)

1. Lawrence J. Ellison, Oracle ($192.9 million)
2. Frederick M. Poses, Trane ($127.1 million)
3. Aubrey K. McClendon, Chesapeake Energy ($116.9 million)
4. Angelo R. Mozilo, Countrywide Financial ($102.8 million)
5. Howard D. Schultz, Starbucks ($98.6 million)
6. Nabeel Gareeb, MEMC Electronic Mats ($79.6 million)
7. Daniel P. Amos, AFLAC ($75.1 million)
8. Lloyd Blankfein, Goldman Sachs Group ($73.7 million)
9. Richard D. Fairbank, Capital One Financial ($73.17 million).
10. Bob R. Simpson, XTO Energy ($72.3 million)

Source: "Special Report: CEO Compensation," *Forbes*, 2008.

Source: Adapted from *The Growing Divide: Inequality and the Roots of Economic Insecurity Trainer's Manual*, 2009.

The Ten Chairs Activity

Facilitator's Goals

a. Define and compare the concepts of "wealth" and "income."
b. Dramatize wealth inequality and the dramatic shift in wealth from 1979 to 2007.
c. Demonstrate the disparity of wealth distribution by race.
d. Use humor and have fun while learning about a serious topic.

The first part of this activity (see Instruction 1) establishes the difference between wealth and income so that participants will have a solid frame of reference as they experience the dramatic Ten Chairs activity that follows. With a lot of time, the discussion about wealth and income can happen in pairs or small groups first, and then a sample of responses can be shared.

The Ten Chairs activity portrays the distribution of household wealth in the U.S. in 2007 between the top 10% and everyone else and the dramatic growth in wealth for the top 1%—and engages participants in dialogue about wealth inequality. It works best with chairs that don't have armrests. The chairs can be lined up across the front of the room facing the participants, prior to the start of the activity. Each chair represents 10% of all the private wealth in the United States. Each of 10 volunteer participants represents 10% of the population of the U.S. It is helpful to identify one person who is willing to represent the "top 10%" who may have a sense of humor or theatrical qualities (i.e., a "ham"). This activity strives for dialogue between the facilitator and the volunteers in their roles, as well as dialogue and reflection among all the participants. Remember to encourage a round of applause for all the volunteers at the end of this activity.

Instructions

1. Listen to this standard (economist's) definition of wealth [see the first Q & A in the box below]. Name examples of assets that low-income, middle-income, and upper-income people might have. [The facilitator can note that there are other ways to view wealth, and participants can be asked to share alternative definitions, e.g., "a person can be considered rich in education, experience, influence, children, etc."]

What Is Wealth?

Questions: How is wealth different from income? What is wealth?

Answers: Wealth is private assets minus liabilities (debt). Simply put, wealth is what you own minus what you owe. Income is your paycheck or government benefit check or dividend check, or your profit from selling an investment, etc. Wealth is what you have in the bank and the property and investments you own.

Question: Is it possible to have negative wealth?

Answer: Yes. Seventeen percent of the U.S. population in 2007 had no assets or negative assets; they owed more than they owned.

Question: What are examples of assets that lower income people might have?

Answer: Cash (savings or checking account), furniture, a car.

Question: What are examples of assets owned by middle-income people?

Answer: Cash (savings or checking account), equity in a house, a small business, a little bit of stock, and/or a retirement fund.

Question: What are examples of assets owned by the top 1%?

Answer: Real estate, large stock and bond holdings, businesses, artwork, and other collectibles.

2. Let's have ten volunteers stand in front of one of the chairs. We need one person who is willing to be the "top 10%." [Remember to try and select a person who is a bit of a ham.] Each person represents one-tenth of the U.S. population, and each chair represents one-tenth of all the private material wealth in the United States. If wealth were evenly distributed, this is what it would look like—one person, one chair. [One variation is to have each person sit in a chair while the facilitator makes the point that this picture of equal wealth distribution has never existed. When folks have to give up their chairs, it ups the emotional punch of the activity.]

3. Currently (the most up-to-date data we have is for 2007), the top 10% owns 71% of all private wealth. The volunteer representing the top 10% takes over seven chairs, "evicting" the current occupants and making himself comfortable on his expanded share of the wealth pie. The rest of the volunteers (representing 90% of the U.S. population) must share three chairs (about 30% of the wealth pie). [This may require some shepherding and encouragement. Groups less familiar with one another will cluster, sitting and standing around the chairs.]

4. Even within the top 10% there is great disparity—a disparity that has increased significantly over the three decades. In 1976 the share of the top 1% was 22% (about two chairs). But by 2007, their share had increased to 34% of all wealth (3½ chairs)! That's as big a piece of the wealth pie as the bottom 90% have combined! [To illustrate this, the facilitator can let the arm of the volunteer representing the top 10% represent the wealthiest 1% of the households, or you can use a top hat or other prop representing ostentatious wealth.]

5. Notice the circumstances you are in and your own feelings about this. How are you feeling at the top? How about in the bottom 90%? If you were going to push someone off the chairs to make room, who would it be? Why? What conclusions do you draw about the focus of public policy discussions—looking up the chairs (at the top 1%) or looking down the chairs at the disadvantaged? What questions do you have? [Often folks direct their anger at the person representing the top 10%. Yet in reality this group remains largely invisible to the rest while wedges based on race, gender, sexual orientation, age, and class are driven between folks, and we all battle each other for more space on the few remaining chairs.]

Source: Adapted from *The Growing Divide: Inequality and the Roots of Economic Insecurity Trainer's Manual*, 2009.

Agenda	Facilitator Role	Investigator Role	Learning Process
Study wealth and access to power.	Have the group read and discuss each section. Remind the investigators to make notes about new information that is meaningful to them.	Read and discuss each section.	This information builds naturally on the previous exercises and is a good way to wrap up the "outdoor" activities. Power is an important theme in Getting Ahead. One goal is to open the door for Getting Ahead graduates to the rooms where decisions are made.
Make mental models for what life is like in middle class and wealth.	Have the group read and discuss the case studies of economic class. Set up the development of the two mental models. Have the group add the mental models to the collection.	Create a Mental Model of Middle Class and a Mental Model of Wealth.	The exercises in this module lead up to a better understanding of the environments of middle class and wealth. See below for an optional or additional way to process the mental models.

This section is part of a long learning process in Module 4 that most groups enjoy. The important things for you as a facilitator are to make each step relevant and not "telegraph" your opinions to the group members. The analysis they do as a group and as individuals will lead to their own learning. We don't have to teach because we aren't expecting the investigators to come to "correct" answers.

Additional/optional activity: In Appendix 4 you'll find an activity titled "Newspapers and Magazines—Understanding How Economic Disparity Affects Us Concretely and Abstractly." You'll need to bring daily newspapers and some periodicals.

Below are icons of the Mental Models of Middle Class and Wealth. These are not to be shared with the group but are to give you an idea of what has evolved out of many Getting Ahead groups and the work of Bridges consultants.

most abstract? How much time for the abstract is there in poverty, middle class, and wealth? How do time and attention to the abstract benefit someone?

2. **Powerless and powerful:** What are the forms of power that each class has? Where do people of different classes meet or interact? How can the powerless gain power?

3. **Instability and stability:** How does each class experience instability and stability? How much does stability in daily life matter?

4. **Relationship-based, achievement-based, and connection-based:** Why might people in poverty be more likely to be relationship-based? Why would people in middle class be more likely to be achievement-based? Why connections in wealth? What happens when people from poverty who are relationship-based and

Source: Developed by Phil DeVol, 2004.

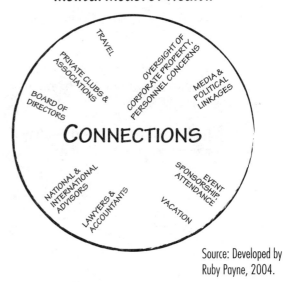

Source: Developed by Ruby Payne, 2004.

These mental models can be used to compare and contrast the three class environments. The following questions go beyond what is found in the *Getting Out* workbook. Their use is optional:

1. **Concrete and abstract:** How much time is there in each circle for abstract activities? Which experience is the most concrete? The

people in middle class who are achievement-based meet? Where do they meet? What expectations do they have of each other? Is an achievement-based approach "better" than a relationship-based approach? What are the benefits of each?

5. **Reactive problem solvers and proactive problem solvers:** In poverty people have to solve problems on the fly, immediately, with the people and tools they have at hand. They use

reactive problem-solving skills. There may not be the time or the resources to do much planning. Where does reactive problem solving tend to lead? Where does proactive problem solving usually lead?

6. **Financial insecurity and financial security:** What is the most important impact on a family of not having financial security? How much financial security is needed to have the kind of life you want?

7. **Tyranny of the moment (short view) and the long view:** How far out in time can you make a plan and be fairly sure it will be done? Can you think past today, next week, next month, or next year? What is the value of living in the moment? What is the value of having the long view?

Can people in poverty:

- Have stability without having financial security?
- Have power without having financial security?
- Have proactive problem-solving approaches without having financial security?
- Think in the abstract without having financial security?
- Work toward achievement without having financial security?
- Have the long view without having financial security?

How would financial security benefit the other aspects of life?

> *We address all causes of poverty.*

The information from the three mental models can begin to feed the investigators' future stories. Remember, the goal of Getting Ahead is not to have people become middle class. What they do with this information is their business. But there are aspects of life that people may learn about that appeal to them. For example, many middle-class people who are deeply rooted in the achievement-based world know that they aren't giving enough time and energy to their family and friends. There are cultures that are more relationship-based than the dominant culture in the U.S.

Agenda	Facilitator Role	Investigator Role	Learning Process
Complete a Personal Chart on Economic Class and write "My Economic Class Story."	Have the investigators go back to the first exercise in this module and look at what they said the causes of poverty were. Ask for their reflections. Introduce the Personal Chart on Economic Class and the assignment to write "My Economic Class Story."	Do the chart during the workshop and write "My Economic Class Story" outside of group time. Put the completed Personal Chart on Economic Class and "My Economic Class Story" into the Future Story Portfolio.	This activity and the economic class stories the investigators write complete the investigation into the causes of poverty and income and wealth disparity. The next step is to see how this information has been used by Getting Ahead graduates and communities.
Introduce the Community Sustainability Grid and the concept of using it as a tool to address all causes of poverty and incarceration	Introduce the Community Sustainability Grid and the concept of using it as a tool to address all causes of poverty. Discuss how the Community Sustainability Grid can be used to take action.	In many Bridges and Getting Ahead communities the grid is used to address poverty in a comprehensive way. Investigators need to know about the grid so they can take part in policy and program development discussions.	Establish that it is necessary to address all the causes of poverty and incarceration—across the four areas of research.
Learn how to use the Community Sustainability Grid.	Encourage the investigators to read the paper in Appendix D of the workbook about how the Community Sustainability Grid has been used. In Appendix 5 of this *User Guide* is a paper titled "Sustainable Communities Where Everyone Can Live Well."	Do some extra reading.	This is a very long and powerful module. The "extra" readings are there for the investigators who have the time and interest in exploring economic class issues more deeply.
Closing	Thank the group members for their hard work.		

NOTES

Module 5

Hidden Rules of Economic Class

Many GA graduates have found great value in the hidden rules. It put into words their cross-class experiences and validated their perceptions. It also gave them tools for analyzing and then navigating new environments. All classes need to know the Bridges and Getting Ahead language, which includes hidden rules, of course. That way there is nothing hidden about the hidden rules!

Agenda	Facilitator Role	Investigator Role	Learning Process
Define the hidden rules of economic class.	Co-investigate the concept of hidden rules by looking at all groups, including those who are incarcerated, not just economic classes.	Participate in the discussion and begin to think about how hidden rules are expressed in films (see Appendix H in the *Getting Out* workbook) and music.	Read about the hidden rules in the paper "Sequence and Reinforcement of Key Concepts Found in Getting Ahead" in Appendix 1. Group members must rely on each other to learn about the hidden rules.
Understand the Key Points that underlie this approach to economic class.	Read through the Key Points with the group, allowing enough time to understand and discuss the points that interest them. Draw particular attention to Key Point 10. That Key Point is the subject of Sequence 3 described in the "Sequence and Reinforcement of Key Concepts Found in Getting Ahead" in Appendix 1.	Take part in the discussion. Make notes about ideas you want to remember. Add those notes to your Future Story Portfolio.	Information about the hidden rules often brings up questions about our approach. The Key Points address many of those questions. This is a good time to learn about the hidden rules of prison life—and for investigators to analyze the rules they live under.

Additional Information on the Key Point About Relationships

In order to achieve anything of significance, an individual may have to give up relationships (at least for a time). This is true for people of all classes and applies to all sorts of achievements. This is especially true for returning citizens. Often it is their old relationships, family, and friends, some of whom may have been part of the criminal activity that led to incarceration. While those people may be the only family and friends the investigator has, reestablishing relationships with these people could be the first step leading to re-offending.

Begin by reading Sequence 3 in the "Sequence and Reinforcement of Key Concepts Found in Getting Ahead" paper in Appendix 1.

One of the unique features of Getting Ahead is that we name and address one of the most difficult issues that people often face when they start moving out of poverty: what to do about relationships that change. Almost everyone who is on that journey has a story to tell about relationships lost, changed, and gained. There are no two stories alike, but there are some themes and lessons learned that can make the experience a little less painful. It certainly helps to know that others face the problem too.

Remember that there's no need to drive home this point right away. The sequencing will give the group several chances to talk about the idea. One GA investigator's reaction to this was immediate and poignant: "If I have to choose between achievement and relationships, I'm going with relationships." It's interesting that she was in college. As the discussion unfolded she shared that her older brother had abandoned the family when he went to college. He left and never came back, and she wasn't going to do that to her family again.

Another investigator's approach was to leave a message on her answering machine that said, "I'm making some changes in my life, and if I don't return your call, you may be one of them." This isn't the recommended way of handling this Key Point, but it does illustrate that everyone finds his/her own solutions.

Part of the sequence is to distinguish between bonding and bridging capital (Module 6) and to develop strategies for building more bridging social capital. There are many things that can be done to support people after they complete Getting Ahead—things that will smooth their journey.

Agenda	Facilitator Role	Investigator Role	Learning Process
Investigate hidden rules, including the hidden rules of incarceration.	Turn the work over to your co-investigators.	Develop an understanding of each hidden rule and provide examples in the chart describing the hidden rules.	Once again, group members turn to each other to learn. They begin to trust each other to take an active part in the learning experience.
Analyze the dynamics of power and public policy.	Review the information in Module 4 about power in preparation for this module's even more extensive discussion of the subject.	Discuss the many aspects of power as they relate to the investigators.	This material is experienced at the individual, institutional, and community/policy levels. Use this as another example of how a full analysis means using the "triple lens."

Additional Information on Studying the Hidden Rules

1. Notice that there's much more information provided here for you about hidden rules than there is in the workbook for the investigators. The work of explaining, illustrating, understanding, and applying the hidden rules is left largely to the investigators. If you encourage the investigators to do "the work of learning," you can act as facilitator rather than teacher.

> 'People who learn to handle their own information flow move from dependency to a sense of control over their future.'
>
> –Daniel Taylor-Ide and Carl Taylor, *Just and Lasting Change: When Communities Own Their Futures*

2. As the facilitator, you will have many opportunities to learn about hidden rules from the investigators themselves before they ever hear of hidden rules. Listen to their conversations from the first day and pick up on the stories that are told about encounters with middle-class people in middle-class settings. If relationships are strained or broken, if feelings are running high, it's quite likely that a hidden rule was broken. Remember (or write down) these stories so you can use them to illustrate hidden rules. Pay particular attention to stories about encounters with guards, social workers, and other employees of the institution.

3. Investigators can look for illustrations of the hidden rules in films, books, and music. Expect them to name a number of rules themselves, but there's a reading and viewing list in the Appendix of the workbook, should they need it. Your role is to reinforce the learning about hidden rules in upcoming modules.

4. You don't have to hit a home run with the hidden rules (or any other concept in Getting Ahead) because the main ideas are sequenced. A home run is when someone presents a concept so thoroughly that all investigators in the workgroup master the concept the first time they hear it. You'll want to reinforce the hidden rules only as they come up naturally. A series of singles, doubles, and even bunts will allow every member of the group to score.

5. You don't have to defend the hidden rules as real or right. In fact, you don't have to defend anything in Getting Ahead. You only have to lead an investigation into the ideas. Some groups have struggled with the hidden rules because they tend to see exceptions to the patterns; emphasize that seeing patterns, not engaging in stereotyping, are the goal. If the group members feel comfortable sharing their own ideas and are not intimidated, they will learn from one another. Investigators will know where they stand regarding the value of the hidden rules as a result of the dialogue. They don't have to come to an agreement about them. The 12 (or whatever number) investigators are not a jury; they don't need to make a unanimous decision.

> 'We all must set our insecurities aside and believe that we all have the ability to make the necessary changes in our lives, enabling us to be an inspiration to all children ... It is easy to settle for living in poverty, but the time has come that we stand up and be noticed.'
>
> –Fannie Carr, GA Graduate,
> South Bend, IN

6. The mental models of class that were created in Modules 1 and 4 are hanging on the wall. Suggest that the investigators use the mental models to help understand where many of the hidden rules come from.

7. Knowledge is power; knowledge of the hidden rules of all three economic classes gives a degree of power to the person who knows them over the person who doesn't. In situations where the organizers of Getting Ahead know the hidden rules and the people in poverty don't, it opens the door to manipulation. Those with the knowledge and the power take action on the "other," the object(s) of the program. This is standard practice of the middle class, and it's just more of the same for people who don't have much power. Getting Ahead is unique because it equips those who are incarcerated and people in poverty with the same information that the dominant class has. This makes it possible to bring the two groups together where they act together, not against one another. This also makes it possible to develop authentic relationships of mutual respect.

8. Our goal is to help the investigators be able to choose which hidden rules to use while building resources. The investigators haven't yet been introduced to resources (that comes in Module 6), but it isn't too early for you to be listening for the connections in their lives between hidden rules and resources. For example, when parents have run-ins with school officials, they often defend their children by attacking the teachers or principal and using the casual register. The hidden rules being used (protecting children and using casual register) actually work against building mental (educational) resources for children. Investigators can discuss the value of using formal-register language to negotiate in order to get support for children from the school system.

9. While investigating the hidden rules, feel free to slip in concrete applications to whet the appetite for more information. For example, Robert Kiyosaki's book *Rich Dad, Poor Dad* has mental models of how people in poverty, middle class, and wealth think about money. These can be taught in just a few minutes. (You don't, however, want this to turn into a long session on money management.) For copyright reasons, we can't provide those mental models here, so interested facilitators will want to buy Kiyosaki's book. The mental models can be found in Chapter 3, Lesson 2 of *Rich Dad, Poor Dad*.

10. When looking into the hidden rule for time, have the investigators draw several mental models for time. This reinforces the theme of "time" in this workbook. We introduced the concept of the tyranny of the moment when we built the Mental Model of Poverty in Module 1, then talked about getting to the abstract in Module 3. Here you can make the point again that people who are stuck in the tyranny of the moment often think and talk about the present and the past, but spend less time or en-

ergy thinking about the future. When you talk about time, it's helpful to draw a time line that shows all three. Let group members come up with models of their own. One group used the "Slinky" as a model for time because of the ups and downs that occur for people at the bottom rungs of the economic ladder. For example, it often takes a student from a low-income family four years to get through a two-year degree program because his/her environment tends to be unstable. Students from a more stable environment can usually get through a four-year degree program in four or five years.

Background Information on How Hidden Rules Can Be Used

Please review these points before leading the discussion about hidden rules. These points are similar to the discussion questions in the *Getting Ahead while Getting Out* workbook.

1. Understanding the hidden rules of economic class can help you if you don't think of them as *right and wrong, good and bad*—as if you have to be *for* or *against* them. It's more helpful to think of them as "guidelines" that children follow almost unconsciously (simply by breathing) when they're growing up. Naturally, they'll keep using many of them in their adult life.

2. One set of rules is not better than another. There is a tendency for people to think that the middle-class rules are better or "right." After all, schools and work operate mostly according to middle-class rules. But the more familiar we are with hidden rules, the more we find that blending them and borrowing rules of another class can be very helpful.

> *People from different classes begin to overcome their own judgmental attitudes and build relationships of mutual respect.*

3. The economic class we're in and the hidden rules we use can be part of how we see ourselves. When we make changes in our lives, we are redefining our identity. That applies as much to changes in our economic status as it does to our education or simple (but not easy) things like switching from being a smoker to a non-smoker. Understanding the hidden rules can help you *if you are aware of the identity issue and if* you don't think of your class as your whole *identity*. If you cling to your hidden rules or class as the definition of who you are, it will be much harder to use them to help yourself and others.

4. Think of the hidden rules as a *choice* or as *the rules of a game*. The more rules you know, the more games you can play. For example, if you want to play basketball, you have to know the rules; you can't tackle people like in football. And you can't play poker if you don't know the rules; without the rules it's just a deck of cards. So ... if you want to do well at work and school, you'll need to know and use middle-class rules. That doesn't mean the rules of poverty are wrong. Use the rules of each class when and where you need to. A woman who is a supervisor in a government agency said, "When I'm at work, I use the middle-class rules. When I'm at home with my friends, I use the poverty rules."

5. Understanding the hidden rules can help you *if you use them to build relationships of mutual respect and if* you don't use them to judge others or to compare yourself to others.

6. Judgments and comparisons happen in all classes. We tend to measure how we're doing compared to our neighbors and friends. Those kinds of comparisons are a form of snobbery. People who get too caught up in constant comparisons live on the "knife's edge" between envy and contempt. We prefer to think in terms of economic security, something we wish for everyone.

7. Unfortunately, people get into conflicts all the time over the hidden rules. One of the best things about this theory is that it gives us a different, less personal way to understand the conflicts. Once we know there are hot spots, we might choose to handle ourselves differently. This will improve our ability to notice and name the conflicts as they happen.

8. Taking responsibility for our workshop experience and our hidden rules is the first step in understanding others. If we don't "own" *our* experiences and hidden rules, we tend to be judgmental and negative about others who aren't like us. Another way of putting this is to think about how people "normalize" their own experience and assume that others see the world in the same way. People from the dominant culture, race, or class are most likely to normalize their experiences because to them the power and status they enjoy tend to be invisible and assumed.

Agenda	Facilitator Role	Investigator Role	Learning Process
Study the impact of poverty and incarceration on families and children.	Using the hidden rule of family structure, introduce the studies (see p. 120 in the workbook) on marriage and children.	Reflect on the data and their meaning to you and the group. Make notes about how you will use this information.	These are difficult and painful studies to learn about. The process of working with them can be discouraging too. By this time the group will probably be in the "performing" stage and will be supporting one another. Where there's difficult material, there's also the opportunity to do something new and positive.
Create a Mental Model of My Family Structure.	Explain the two examples of a family structure.	Create a mental model of your family.	This broadens the conversation and examination of one's family situation and contributes to the sequence about giving up (at least for a period of time) relationships for achievement.

Module 5: Hidden Rules of Economic Class

Additional Information About Families

In Getting Ahead the information about families is spread across several modules. There are two reasons for this: First, as noted in the workbook, most people usually have strong opinions and mental models of what a "proper" family is. Rather than get caught up in political, religious, and social arguments, it's better for us to review important data and examine our own families while leaving space for each person's beliefs. Second, working at family issues in connection with multiple modules allows us to look at families through the economic lens, touching on it with a lighter but very relevant touch when we do.

Remember, family issues, like everything else, will come up in the self-assessment in Module 8. That is where investigators will have an opportunity to examine resources involving at least the following four factors: emotional, spiritual, social capital, and relationships/role models. As the facilitator, you will want to suspend your own attitudes and convictions about families—and resist the urge to impose your "solutions."

The information on families and children can be painful for some people, but it also can be hopeful. It's a *weiji* moment for some investigators. *"Weiji"* is the Chinese word for crisis: *Wei* is the danger represented by any crisis, and *ji* is the opportunity that may present itself. For example, it may be painful and risky to decide that someone has to leave your house, someone who isn't good for you or your children. The opportunity is that you can create the future story you want. It's easier to face the crisis in a group that is nonjudgmental and safe—and where you can find support—than it is alone or with people who tend to give mixed messages. Let the group do the work of challenging one another; your role is to be there to make it safe for everyone.

Agenda	Facilitator Role	Investigator Role	Learning Process
Create a Time-Management Matrix.	Co-investigate the Time-Management Matrix.	Make sure you and the group members know how to do the matrix. You may have to do this outside of the workgroup. Add the matrix to your Future Story Portfolio.	This is another step toward preparing the investigators for the SMART Plan they will develop in Module 11.
Closing	Remind the group of how many workshop meetings are left. If there's time, go to the Module 9 Community Assessment and start an investigation into neighborhood conditions, using the activities you find there.		

Additional Information About Time Management

There are many opportunities for co-investigators to have an "aha" moment or to suddenly decide to make changes. You will rarely know when that will happen or what it takes for someone to take the risk of doing something new. This exercise might lead to just such a moment. One investigator reported that she was furious with herself when she saw it laid out how she was spending her time.

NOTES

Module 6

Eleven Resources

One of the unique features of Getting Ahead and Bridges is the definition of poverty (taken from Ruby Payne): "the extent to which an individual, institution, or community does without resources." This is important to many GA investigators whose income isn't below the Federal Poverty Guidelines: They feel uncomfortable when the term "poverty" is applied to them. Getting Ahead is generally open to people whose income is 200% of the Federal Poverty Guidelines and sometimes perhaps more.

That's why, throughout the workbook, we use a variety of terms to describe the situations that GA investigators come from: low-income, near poverty, low-wage, and people living in unstable situations.

Our definition gives every GA investigator something to do about his/her personal situation: Identify which resources are low and work at building them.

Agenda	Facilitator Role	Investigator Role	Learning Process
Define poverty.	Co-investigate the way poverty is defined in Getting Ahead and Bridges.	Participate in the discussion.	In earlier modules we used the term "resources" (financial resources, for example). Now we're using the term in the definition of poverty. Resources constitute the center of the *Getting Out* workbook. The focus on resources becomes more intense as we work toward the plan to build resources.
Define the 11 resources.	Introduce the definitions. In addition to language (Module 2) and hidden rules (Module 5), six resources are described in some detail. Take them one at a time, stopping to discuss them as needed. If additional case studies are needed, find them in the book *Bridges Out of Poverty*.	Take part in the readings and in discussing the resources.	Review the Mental Model of Poverty and add "resources" as another analytical category, if it isn't there already.
Create a Mental Model of Social Capital.	Introduce the activity.	Create a Mental Model of Social Capital. Investigate bridging social capital and networking skills. Add it to the Future Story Portfolio.	The idea of social capital was introduced earlier. Now we add the terms "bridging" and "bonding" to social capital. Networking skills introduced in this module can be of help in Module 10, "Building Resources." This is in recognition of the importance of social capital.

continued on next page

continued from previous page

Agenda	Facilitator Role	Investigator Role	Learning Process
Use case studies to practice doing an assessment of resources.	Set up an analysis of the two case studies. Do additional case studies found in the book *Bridges Out of Poverty,* if the group needs to practice some more.	Analyze the case studies, scoring each resource on the 5-point scale.	This might be seen as practice for the next module when the investigators will do a self-assessment. Explore ways to use this information.
Explore ways to use this information.	Read and discuss the book *The R Rules.*	Participate in the discussion about *The R Rules.*	It's logical and natural that investigators will begin using the information they have been discovering. The point is that this information can be used immediately—and it can be used deliberately and intentionally.
Plan backwards.	Co-investigate how to plan backwards, using examples given to illustrate the process.	Practice planning backwards with concrete action items in your life.	Planning backwards is part of the plans that will be made in Module 11.

Additional Information About How Investigators Can Use Their Knowledge of Resources

- Up until now we've been co-investigating research and hidden rules, which are systemic issues and often broad generalizations. Some GA investigators find relief in those modules because they learned that poverty was not just about them, that large systemic factors were and are at work.

  But the issues of identity and belonging can be troubling and painful. Some people want to join the mainstream or dominant culture, others want to dismantle or change the system, and everyone struggles with what to do about relationships as they begin to change.

- In this module you'll be introducing a core concept, a foundational component of this work. This is where we define poverty and prosperity. What is learned now will be used to make plans at the end of the workbook.

- Resources can be defined as quality-of-life indicators. Intuitively, taking the 11 resources as a whole, it's better to have high resources than low resources. It's important to say that high quality of life doesn't depend on having high financial resources, but it's also fair to say that being financially stable reduces stress and brightens the future.

Module 6: Eleven Resources

> *'Choose not to sell yourself short; living in poverty is no one's destiny.'*
>
> —GA Graduate

- Returning citizens in unstable situations and in poverty tend to (but don't always) have lower resources than others. In fact, that is one definition of poverty (as noted above): the extent to which a person does without resources. This is made easier to understand and accept when we remember the Mental Model of Poverty we created in Module 1. Being poor means we're vulnerable to daily fears and problems, to the extent that we're living in the tyranny of the moment. We don't have enough time to solve all the daily problems, let alone build financial, emotional, mental, or social resources.

- So assessing the resources of individuals is difficult—even painful—to do. This is about the individual, and every GA investigator will have a different story, different strengths, and different weaknesses. This is very different from the typical agency assessment experience where people were likely to be defined as "needy and deficient" and handed a treatment plan. In Getting Ahead the investigators assess their own resources.

- But first, in this module, the GA investigators will be scoring (assessing) case studies. We do this because we want to practice using the concepts we'll use later when we do a *self*-assessment regarding our own resources.

    a. The chart titled "Resources Scoring Chart," which appears in Module 6, introduces five categories for each resource. These categories range from "Urgent/Crisis" to "Thriving/Giving Back." They're numbered 1 to 5, where 1 is low and 5 is high. In Module 8 these definitions and scoring mechanisms will appear in the self-assessment in an expanded format. Take a moment to go to Module 8 to see the expanded version of this chart. You'll notice that for each box in this chart there's a series of statements. You don't need to use the detailed scoring statements of Module 8 here in Module 6, but it's important that you know that we're introducing an idea and process here that will be reinforced later.

    b. For additional case studies, use the scenarios from Chapter 1 in *Bridges Out of Poverty* or case studies that you create in order to practice the scoring of resources.

- *Always* focus on the strengths a person has within each resource and across all resources. After all, it's upon *strengths* that plans for economic stability are built.

- Most investigators tend to make sweeping (sometimes oversimplified) appraisals of the case studies and their own resources. To confront a GA investigator's appraisals is too much like school, with all of its "right" answers. It would be better to work over the material several times, using more and more precise questions, to help investigators make accurate assessments of their own resources.

- If or when members of the group get stuck—when they're caught up in their feelings, looking down, growing silent, or getting defensive—name what it is you see and ask if they want a break, a time to reflect, in order to clear the air. Once the problem is defined, work for a solution that will allow the group to get back to work. If that isn't possible, create a plan with the group to address the problem, *then* get back to work.

- Remind the group of the time line. The group will be meeting 20 times. How many workshop meetings remain? This is important because it illustrates how to think of time, and it begins to work toward closure.

Module 7
Threat Assessment

The first 72 hours after release from incarceration is a very dangerous period for returning citizens. Knowing that fact led to the idea of developing a 72-Hour Stability Plan for all investigators. That way when they walk out the door they will have a plan in hand. The 72-Hour Stability Plan should, whenever possible, be shared with family, friends, and allies in the community, as well as with the Releasing Authority.

This module asks the investigators to do an inventory of themselves that will identify any of their thinking and behavior that can sabotage them in the first few hours. Using the inventory, the investigators will build the 72-Hour Stability Plan in Module 11.

This activity will create a series of 10 trend lines covering 10 areas of life. The trend lines show the ups and downs of life—highlighting key experiences, actions, decisions, and consequences. The last table is a summary of the 10 and usually reveals patterns of events, thinking, and behaviors.

Agenda	Facilitator Role	Investigator Role	Learning Process
Review data on causes of recidivism and discuss the dangers faced in the first 72 hours after release.	Introduce the investigation and facilitate the discussion.	Participate in the discussion.	This module sets up the need for the 72-Hour Stability Plan.
Do the activity called Discovering Patterns in My LIfe.	During the discussion about the activity, focus on the things that individuals can control, particularly thinking patterns. Acknowledge the reality of systemic barriers in the community and bring the conversation back to what can be done starting now, while they are still incarcerated.	Do the activity.	Many offenders have been through "Thinking for Change," an evidence-based program that is very intense. This activity can support what was learned there.
Write a paper titled "My Threat Assessment."	Invite investigators to share their "My Threat Assessment" paper at the next session. Explain that the 72-Hour Stability Plan will be created in Module 11.	Write the paper. Sharing the paper with others is optional.	Discussion about the papers can lead to new learning from others and help strengthen the 72-Stability Plan.

Module 8

Self-Assessment of Resources

Now the Getting Ahead investigators consider their own experience, their concrete reality, in light of what they have been learning. The mental models, activities, investigations, reflections, and conversations at the "kitchen table" are all brought to bear in this personal assessment.

Agenda	Facilitator Role	Investigator Role	Learning Process
Do a Self-Assessment of Resources.	Review what has been covered in Getting Ahead to remind the group of how much work has gone into this module. Have GA investigators work independently. Provide someone to read the assessment to anyone who can't read well.	Perform a Self-Assessment of Resources.	This activity draws upon all the preceding information. It now forms the foundation for the remainder of the workshop. In Module 9, GA investigators will consider what the community can offer them and also what they might contribute to the community (as an individual or as part of a group). The assessment of resources helps investigators determine which ones are priorities. This will assist the discussion in Module 10 on building resources.
Create a Mental Model of Resources.	Set up the activity.	Create the bar chart representing resources. Place the self-assessment in the Future Story Portfolio.	The assessment will provide information for GA investigators' Personal Plan for Building Resources—for both the resources to target and the resources that might support the development of others.
Closing	Celebrate the hard work.	Celebrate the work well done.	

Additional Information About Self-Assessment

The Getting Ahead investigators know the importance of this module. Some people will be apprehensive about it, even dreading it. Some will be eager to do it, and a few may have already done it. In the latter case, ask them to do it again.

Remind group members of the following:

- This evaluation is based on the work they have done so far. Review the mental models that they have created. Celebrate the hard work they've done!

- They did solid, tight thinking during the analysis of case studies and when studying their own lives. That same objective, honest approach is needed now.

- The plans they create will be based on the information that comes from this self-assessment. If the information isn't accurate or true, the plans won't make sense or be worth much. This is exactly what we found in Module 1 when we made the Mental Model of Poverty: If the information about poverty isn't accurate or true, the plans made by organizations and the community won't be worth the paper they're written on.

- The self-assessment can be painful. It will take courage, persistence, and support from one's friends to see it through. They are not alone; they have the backing of the group

Some reminders for the facilitator:

- People who are currently incarcerated or have been released are likely to have a number of low resources. Some individuals in test groups went through the process, looked at their low scores, and began to revise them upward (note that the procedural steps speak directly to this). Encourage GA investigators to resist the urge to "improve" their scores, focusing instead on intellectual detachment and objectivity, the same skills necessary to create realistic future plans.

- Remind the investigators that no matter how many of their resources are low, in Module 10 they will learn how to build resources.

- This is another point in the sequence (see Appendix 1) where GA investigators might express their motivation for change. It can be very personal and quite painful. One woman reported that she went to the restroom and wept for 20 minutes before returning with a determination to build her own resources and those of her children. At this point group members also might be supporting each other in various ways outside of the workshop setting.

- It's important to allow investigators time to process their feelings—sometimes alone, sometimes with others (including the facilitator)—before moving on to the community assessment. If the processing doesn't happen, they won't be much good when trying to assess the community. Some of this processing needs to happen at the end of the self-assessment workshop. Another opportunity to debrief (briefly) should be offered at the start of Module 9.

- The self-assessment is used by GA graduates to monitor their progress. From the earliest groups we've heard that most GA grads just naturally redo the self-assessment every so often to see how they're doing.

- The self-assessment is embedded in the evaluation tools provided by SupplyCore Technology Group's MPOWR evaluation tool and Charity Tracker described in Appendix 7. If the sponsor or community invests in the SupplyCore evaluation, the investigator will see the same questions in the MPOWR instrument.

NOTES

Module 9
Community Assessment

In this module Getting Ahead investigators will do two assessments and develop two mental models about the community. One mental model is for the community, while the other is for them.

1. The Community Assessment Mental Model uses typical quality-of-life indicators, as well as indicators based on GA to describe conditions in the community that pertain to returning citizens, the working poor, and people in or near poverty.

2. The One-on-One Relationships Mental Model identifies the individuals and groups in the community (associations and organizations) where the investigator and the groups both act to build resources and solve problems.

The work done in this module will feed the thinking about where and how to build resources. The information also can be shared with the community by the GA investigators. This can be done in a way that emphasizes the value their point of view, their insights, and their credibility.

Agenda	Facilitator Role	Investigator Role	Learning Process
Investigate the community for its ability to provide a high-quality life for everyone, including people in poverty and near poverty, as well as returning citizens.	As suggested in earlier modules, you may have started this investigation earlier. Have the Getting Ahead investigators work alone or in teams to assess the nine areas of study (see *Getting Ahead while Getting Out* workbook).	Gather information from past experiences, personal knowledge, and information from family and friends.	The theme of the two story lines shifts back to the community.
Complete a Community Assessment Mental Model.	Challenge the group to do thorough and solid work. Do not defend organizations that are criticized; just ask for thorough investigations. The Community Assessment Mental Model goes on the wall with the other mental models.	Share results of the investigation and work with the rest of the group to assign a 1–5 value to the bar chart.	This mental model holds information that planners and decision makers in the institutions and community need. Here is where GA investigators may begin to understand both their value as poverty experts and the power of their own voices.

Additional Information About the Community Assessment Mental Model

- Poverty is experienced differently in every community and country. In Module 1 you created a Mental Model of Poverty that was based on local conditions. This information is valuable because it is local information provided by local experts. The GA investigators' credibility comes from their direct knowledge of life in unstable situations and poverty. Their credibility is increased when they use what they have learned in Getting Ahead to interact with people from middle class and wealth. Increasingly, GA graduates speak at conferences, participate in meetings, and serve on boards.

- Investigators will gather information from their own knowledge of the community, from friends and family living in the community, and/or from other inmates who recently lived in the community. Inmates who have access can use the correctional facility's library to gather information by reading newspapers or other material available to them, as well as using the Internet to obtain information (as permitted by the correctional facility).

- The Community Assessment Mental Model is a bar chart (see p. 214 of workbook) that presents the conclusions quickly. More detailed information from the study will have to be presented.

- Provide information about the methodology.

- Make it interesting.

Agenda	Facilitator Role	Investigator Role	Learning Process
Identify community assets (individuals, associations, and institutions) that can help Getting Ahead investigators build resources. Create a Group One-on-One Relationships Mental Model.	Use the Community Assets Map to help organize the investigation. Work with the GA investigators to decide on the areas of interest, the scope of the investigations, and the methods. The Group One-on-One Relationships Mental Model goes onto the wall and into the collection of mental models that can be shared with the community. This is an opportunity to build social capital.	Decide on the groups and individuals who will be investigated. Divide up the work. Do the investigations and report back to the workgroup. Help create the Group One-on-One Relationships Mental Model. Focus on people whom you want to be on your support team; practice networking skills.	The GA investigators will have to apply the new things they have learned in order to conduct this investigation. This includes knowledge of different economic class environments, hidden rules, definition of resources, language issues, and the intention to solve community problems.
Create a Personal One-on-One Relationships Mental Model.	Help the investigators visualize how they can create this mental model.	Put your name in the center of the model and create a Personal One-on-One Relationships Mental Model. Add this model to your Future Story Portfolio.	These mental models will feed directly into modules on building resources and making plans.
Closing	Celebrate the group's work. Work with the group to plan the graduation celebration and the other "post-Getting Ahead" suggestions in Appendix A in the *Getting Out* workbook.	Start working on the graduation celebration.	

Additional Information About the Personal One-on-One Relationships Mental Model

- This module allows the GA investigators to assess specific community conditions and work together to build a mental model of the community's resources. The information is personalized by having the group members investigate the associations and institutions based on their own interests.

- This is an opportunity for GA investigators to become problem solvers in the community. For example, they may choose to advocate for improved housing, better paying jobs, or fair credit opportunities—or to become facilitators for United for a Fair Economy. They also may choose to partner with middle-class people on issues like transportation and predatory lending. In addition, GA investigators may want to become your co-facilitator for the next Getting Ahead workshop.

Getting Ahead graduates have acted as consultants to courts, hospitals, and other organizations that need poverty experts.

Goals include:

a. To identify people from middle class for potential partnerships

b. To identify people who will become your support team after you complete Getting Ahead (see the Mental Model of Support that will be created in Module 11)

c. To assist GA investigators, who want to become involved, in getting to the decision-making tables in the community

NOTES

Module 10
Building Resources

Facilitators might think of Getting Ahead as a very large mediation process. You will recall from Module 2 on language that mediation identifies the stimulus (the *what*), the meaning (the *why*), and the response (the *how*). Investigators learn how to do mediation with their children, but it's also part of the design of Getting Ahead.

The *what* in Getting Ahead includes the mental models of economic class, the Mental Model of My Life upon Release, causes of poverty and mass incarceration, and the impact that both have have on families.

The *why* comes from creating a future story and developing the motivation to move from the current life to a better life. That crucial shift comes from the module on change, through thought and analysis, and (most importantly) from the conversations at the "kitchen table."

The *how* comes from the modules on resources, hidden rules, language, and assessments. They feed GA investigators' ideas on how the changes can take place. Indeed, this is the module where the concrete strategies for building resources are developed.

Agenda	Facilitator Role	Investigator Role	Learning Process
Analyze the difference between resources that are for "getting by" and resources that are for "getting ahead."	Co-investigate the information on resources that are "needs based" versus "power based."	Apply the information on getting-by resources and getting-ahead resources at the personal level.	Understanding the value and purpose of the two ways in which resources are provided in the community will help in planning for the future.
Develop ways to build each resource.	Work through the two activities so that resource-building strategies become concrete.	Work with the group to develop concrete ways to build resources. Add the worksheets to your Future Story Portfolio.	The strategies developed in this module will be a direct help to the GA investigators in Module 11.
Closing	Remind the group that the graduation is coming up. Plans need to be made.		

Additional Information on Getting-By and Getting-Ahead Resources

1. GA grads tell us that finding ways to build resources turns out to be as difficult for institutions and communities as it is for the investigators. Naming this problem gives individuals and communities a way to talk through—and share—the complexities and challenges.

2. We have to honor how hard it will be to build resources. One GA graduate who now facilitates groups said, "I'm never going to stand in line again." Another GA graduate gave up subsidized housing in order to realize her plan. Both of them succeeded, but both of them said it was very hard to do.

3. The transition from the relative stability of getting-by resources to the instability of getting-ahead resources is when GA graduates need the most support.

4. An obvious and helpful approach for this investigation would be to have representatives of local organizations from the inmates' home communities come in and do presentations for the GA investigators.

   a. GA investigators will often know about the agencies because they have been to them. In fact, they will know which counselors, case managers, or staff members are good and can be trusted.

   b. Often the GA investigators find that there's no community directory—or it's out of date. This may lead to the impulse to create or modify the directory. Encourage them to resist the urge! That is the work of local providers, not GA investigators.

   c. Returning citizens who have been incarcerated for a period of time may no longer be aware of the agencies in the community they are returning to. They may need assistance with housing, employment, child support, driver's licenses, and a host of other issues. The GA investigators should be asked about agencies and help they will need upon their release. The GA investigators should decide which agencies they wish to hear from. The facilitators should then contact those agencies and ask representatives to attend one of the last classes to explain their programs to the investigators. The benefit of this is the investigators meeting agency people and the agency people meeting the investigators. As a result, there is a stronger possibility that the returning citizens will be able to obtain the services they need upon their release. So the goal is for real conversations to take place between the GA investigators and agency personnel. No more than three or four agencies should attend this class.

5. A good test of the ideas that are developed during this module would be to ask, "Have you gotten enough ideas about building 'X' resource that you can see a way to do it?" And: "What would the first steps be?"

> 'More recently we have realized that well-being comes from a process, not from a specific answer. It is the overall journey that determines the direction and length of our steps, not the other way around.'
>
> –Daniel Taylor-Ide and Carl Taylor, *Just and Lasting Change: When Communities Own Their Futures*

NOTES

Module 11
Personal and Community Plans

Everything in Getting Ahead points to the action phase of the work. The last step before that is to create plans, one for each of the two GA themes—individual and community.

The planning process itself can be hard work, but it must be done. More exciting are the last two mental models: My Future Story and Community Prosperity.

Agenda	Facilitator Role	Investigator Role	Learning Process
Review the mental models and investigations that we've done so far. List your highest and lowest resources. Rank the resources you need to work on.	There are blank planning worksheets at the end of Module 11 in the *Getting Ahead while Getting Out* workbook and in Appendix G of the workbook. Have group members review and reflect on everything they have done, using their Future Story Portfolios.	Review the mental models, as well as the time and planning activities. Participate in helping all group members complete the steps.	All the elements of Getting Ahead come together at this time. By this time the GA investigators have taken charge of their learning and can be expected to go at the work with interest, even enthusiasm. The investigators may be struggling with feelings about the impending conclusion of the workshop.
Develop plans for building the resources selected. Create immediate action steps and close the "back doors."	Provide feedback to investigators who ask for it, but don't judge the work of the investigators.	Work at this on your own unless you want feedback from other investigators and/or the facilitator.	The Planning Backwards exercise also may help investigators determine the order of action steps. The "back door" concept will be new for most investigators. However, it is regarded by many GA graduates as a key part of their plans. It's consistent with the relapse prevention and maintenance in the Stages of Change (Module 3).
Create the 72-Hour Stability Plan.	Remind the investigators of the importance of the first hours of their release.	Using the activity provided, develop a personal plan that can be shared with friends and family.	This plan is built on the analysis done in Module 7.
Create SMART (Specific, Measurable, Attainable, Realistic, and Time-specific) goals.	Suggest that one of their SMART goals be one they can work on prior to release; that will help them get ahead upon being released.	Work through the steps of your own plan; assist others only if asked.	Reminder: SMART goals were introduced during the Planning Backwards exercise in Module 6.

continued on next page

continued from previous page

Agenda	Facilitator Role	Investigator Role	Learning Process
Complete the Support for Change Mental Model.	Reflect on the discussion that the group has had on this topic.	Discuss the importance of relationships as you move to the action phase. Create the Personal Support for Change Mental Model.	This is the end piece of a long learning sequence about relationships. Relationships have been named and analyzed in activities and discussions. The support team developed here is a concrete tool that moves to the action phase with the GA investigator.
Create a Mental Model of My Future Story. As a group, create a Mental Model of Community Prosperity. Complete the Future Story Portfolio.	Provide the usual markers and supplies so investigators can exercise their creativity. Using information in "Getting Started (on Your Future Story)" in Appendix A of the *Getting Ahead while Getting Out* workbook, discuss what the GA investigators would like to do as follow-up, including plans for sharing findings with groups in the community to which they're returning. For investigators who will not be released in the near future, discuss the possibilities of continuing to meet monthly to support the plans they have made.	Do the Mental Model of My Future Story and participate in developing the Mental Model of Community Prosperity. Add the worksheets and mental models from this module to your Future Story Portfolio.	You can trust in the creativity of the GA investigators and the group to create meaningful mental models. The GA investigators will need to decide how they will interact with the sponsoring organizations and community at large.
Closing	Work with the group on graduation celebrations and next steps in the community.	Continue to develop specific next steps with co-investigators and the community. Make graduation celebration plans and decide on your level of participation in the community with regard to poverty issues.	The group has been talking about making the transition to "post-Getting Ahead."

Additional Information About Creating the SMART Plan and Mental Models

- By this time most GA investigators have a good idea of what they want to do. This step will formalize their thinking. Others may use this material to decide what their next steps will be.

- Selecting the highest and lowest resources is a matter of moving information from the Self-Assessment Mental Model or bar chart to the charts in the *Getting Ahead while Getting Out* workbook. Identifying the strong resources that can be used to help build weaker resources isn't difficult. But deciding which resource to focus on isn't as straightforward as it may seem. When an investigator is struggling with a choice or priorities, he/she may need some help from other GA investigators.

- One powerful way of illustrating My Future Story is to combine it with the My Life upon Release Mental Model. This puts the mental model of today's reality right beside the mental model of the future. Investigators who have done this have typically put My Life upon Release on the left side of the page and My Future Story on the right.

Getting Started—After Graduation

Group decisions about next steps:

The expectation has always been that the GA investigators would produce information in the form of mental models to share with the community. This is a moment to celebrate. It is when their voices will be heard. The GA group members need to decide how they will present that information and how they might interact with their community, as well as the organizations that sponsored Getting Ahead. In Appendix A of the workbook, "Getting Started (on Your Future Story)" contains information for the investigators to review.

> 'As we went through the Getting Ahead workbook, something happened to both of us. I can't speak for my husband, but I know my whole outlook on my situation changed. It was one of the hardest things I had to do and definitely the most beneficial. You figure out what you need to do and how you need to do it—and then you do it. The book and program are just your tools to use. They are not the hands behind the tools doing all the work.'
>
> –Mary Gruza,
> Graduate and Facilitator,
> Inkster, MI

Appendix

1. Sequence and Reinforcement of Key Concepts Found in Getting Ahead

2. Getting Ahead—the Purpose of Each Module

3. Model Fidelity Elements for Conducting the Getting Ahead Workshop

4. Activity: Newspapers and Magazines—Understanding How Economic Disparity Affects Us Concretely and Abstractly

5. Sustainable Communities Where Everyone Can Live Well

6. Maslow's Hierarchy of Needs

7. Data Collection, Evaluations, Research, and Social Capital

8. Websites

9. Glossary of Terms Used in Corrections and This *User Guide*

Appendix 1
Sequence and Reinforcement of Key Concepts Found in Getting Ahead

by Philip E. DeVol, Author, *Getting Ahead in a Just-Gettin'-By World* and Co-author, *Getting Ahead while Getting Out*

Purpose: The purpose of this paper is to help facilitators become aware of the learning sequences embedded in Getting Ahead (hereafter often referred to as GA) and to encourage facilitators to use them to deepen the learning experience for the investigators.

Audience: "Sequence and Reinforcement of Key Concepts Found in Getting Ahead" is for facilitators who are familiar with GA. It's assumed that the facilitator has read *Getting Ahead while Getting Out,* this *User Guide,* and *Bridges Out of Poverty.* Facilitators also are encouraged to familiarize themselves with resources found on the Getting Ahead website: *www.gettingahead.com.*

Importance of sequencing and reinforcement: When facilitators sequence and reinforce information through activities, discussions, and the use of mental models, it won't be necessary to "teach" or to "hit a home run" with any concept the first time it appears in the workbook. It's important to know that sequencing and reinforcement are running in the background, behind the scenes. For that reason, it's important that a facilitator do each module in the order it appears in the workbook and not skip modules. People who have completed GA have referred to the learning process as layered, something that goes deeper the farther you progress.

Sequence: Knowing the sequence of certain ideas, the facilitator can consciously attend to covering the content at each encounter. There is no need to "telegraph" the sequences to the investigators. It's better for the facilitator to set the process in motion but allow the learners to discover the connections for themselves.

Reinforcement: Linking the learning to previous content need not be formalized either, but instead let it evolve as a natural outgrowth of the investigations. The collection of mental models that hang on the walls in the order of their development can be used by the group to label and record new thoughts on former ideas.

The importance of dialogue: Experience tells us that investigators learn as much or more from the dialogue that arises from the activities as from the activities themselves. The activities are designed to spark reflection and discussions. Discussion time is on equal footing with the exercises or activities. Facilitators will want to pay attention to the balance between content and discussion, keeping them about even.

Format: There are five sequences described here. The first three sequences below are described module by module because they unfold over several modules. The remaining two, while just as important, are described briefly. When facilitators weave the sequences together skillfully, the learning experiences become more powerful. These sequences will tend to work naturally when the investigators can discuss their insights thoroughly.

SEQUENCE 1: Income and Wealth Disparity and the Hidden Rules of Class

Explanation: In short, income and wealth disparity leads to distinct differences in the way people experience life in the United States. These environments (Mental Models of Poverty, Middle Class, and Wealth) give rise to the hidden rules of each class. Knowledge of the hidden rules helps people develop relationships of mutual respect, as well as resolve conflicts. These understandings also help investigators build resources and participate fully on planning and decision-making boards.

Module	Content: Mental Models and Activities	Meaning (Explaining the Links) and Tips
1	Mental Model of Poverty	The very first mental model defines what poverty is like locally. It establishes the idea of class environments. *Tip:* Label it accurately. Following group discussion, put the analytical terms—such as *instability, concrete, relationships, tyranny of the moment, financial security,* and *problem solving*—around the Mental Models of Poverty and My Life upon Release.
4	Investigate Income and Wealth Disparity Create Mental Models of Middle Class and Wealth	Where there's extreme disparity in income and wealth in a nation, there will be sharp differences in the way people experience life in that country. These two mental models, plus the one on poverty created in Module 1, make up the three environments of class. *Tip:* Compare and contrast the three environments of economic class and put key analytical terms on the mental models.
5	Hidden Rules of Class	The hidden rules of class evolve out of the environments of class (the three mental models), which in turn derive from income and wealth disparity. *Tip:* Listen to the stories told by investigators from the very first day in order to pick up examples of hidden rules that are used and broken in their neighborhood and community. These can be used to illustrate the hidden rules.
6	Definition of Poverty Mental Model of Social Capital	The many causes of poverty and the instability it generates make it difficult to maintain resources or to build them. The Mental Model of Social Capital establishes the degree to which an individual has *bonding* and *bridging* capital. This sequence opens a space for investigators to see the value of relationships with individuals from all economic classes, to find the people with whom they have relationships of mutual respect, and to see the possibility of establishing new relationships using their new learning. *Tip:* Let the *group* make the connection between the hidden rules and the development of bridging social capital: Be an observer of the learning taking place in the group.

continued on next page

continued from previous page

Module	Content: Mental Models and Activities	Meaning (Explaining the Links) and Tips
8	Self-Assessment of Resources	Developing a plan without doing an accurate self-assessment is not useful. The quality of the investigator's plan stems from the quality and honesty of the thinking that goes into the self-assessment. Therefore, it's necessary to practice analyzing resources using the previously investigated case studies. Since a key resource is knowledge of hidden rules, it's also important to focus on how much awareness one has of hidden rules—particularly of other economic classes. The shift from judgments that break relationships to understandings that form relationships brings with it a degree of power and influence. The hidden rules can help investigators navigate the societal systems they encounter. *Tip:* There need not be much discussion during and after the self-assessment. As this can be quite painful, allow some time for the group to provide support to one another. Encourage the group to look to the planning phase that will follow.
9	Community Assessment	Doing a community assessment is in keeping with the "two story" pattern in the workbook: the individual's story and the community's story. Poverty isn't just caused by individual choice and behavior but also by what exists (or doesn't exist) in the community. This reinforces the learning that occurred when developing the mental models of class, the causes of poverty, and the significance of social capital. While some of the assessments may be quite negative, the investigators are likely to see inside organizations they don't trust to people who can be trusted. Identifying key individuals (from diverse backgrounds) reinforces the concept of bridging social capital introduced in Module 6. *Tip:* Taking a thorough look at the community for strengths and weaknesses can reinforce the importance of community as a source for change and resources, as well as a place that needs to make changes that benefit people of all classes.
10	Build Resources and the Support for Change Mental Model in Module 11	The last step in building a plan of action is to create a mental model that identifies the people investigators want on their support team. This can include people from the group itself, friends and family, and those with whom they have bridging social capital. *Tip:* Observe how many of the investigators have used this sequence to create relationships across class lines as a means of addressing poverty in their own community.

SEQUENCE 2: Theory of Change; Building a Future Story

Explanation: Learning and using the Getting Ahead Theory of Change has the potential to free a person from the tyranny of the moment—which is experienced by civilian populations in war, victims of natural disasters, people in persistent poverty, and individuals in economic and medical emergencies.

The Theory of Change gives people the power to engage in metacognition, to think about their own thinking. Individuals can become aware of a focus that is narrowed to the now, to the concrete problem that stares them in the face, that allows them to think in the abstract, to reflect on the future, and to make plans that will free them from the control of the powerful present.

The Theory of Change for GA is presented early in the process so that investigators have enough time to encounter the idea again in later discussions. It is made explicit in Module 3, but the sequence actually begins in Module 1.

Module	Content: Mental Models and Activities	Meaning (Explaining the Links) and Tips
1	**Mental Model of Poverty**	The analysis and labels that are written on the mental models developed in Module 1 will feed the development of the Theory of Change.
	My Life upon Release Mental Model	Group discussion and analysis of the Mental Model of Poverty may generate these terms: *concrete, unstable, relationships, problem solving,* and *tyranny of the moment*.
		Tip: The facilitator can introduce the terms when the concepts are being expressed. They can be added to the vocabulary lists that appear at the end of each module in the workbook.
2	**Theory of Change Mental Model**	The facilitator will draw the mental model on chart paper. That mental model is to appear on the wall with all other mental models.
		The terms developed in Module 1 will be necessary to sequence the ideas.
	Stages of Change	People in poverty are busy solving problems; stopping to analyze the situation (as is done in GA) is difficult to do, so one stays in Pre-Contemplation. Moving through the Stages of Change presupposes that your life is fairly stable. Relapse and failure to maintain the change can be linked to instability and the tyranny of the moment. Knowing this Theory of Change can help someone achieve his/her goals.
		Knowing the Stages of Change can put people in charge of their own changes.
		Tip: Facilitators cannot force someone to be motivated or to change. Facilitators can only support people as they move through the Stages of Change. Investigators will progress in their own way and on their own schedule. The facilitator cannot expect to "herd" a group of investigators through the process together at the same time.

continued on next page

continued from previous page

Module	Content: Mental Models and Activities	Meaning (Explaining the Links) and Tips
4	Predators	Predators take advantage of people (especially those in poverty) because of the following three things that are covered in the Theory of Change. 1) Predators provide concrete solutions for *concrete* problems, and they tend to do it quickly. 2) Predators form *relationships* of understanding and respect (often sham), for example: "I'm here to help you. I understand your need for (fill in the blank) right away." 3) Predators rely on the tyranny of the moment, knowing that if they do the first two effectively, it's very unlikely that the customer will analyze the situation, the contract, or the fine print. *Tip:* This is a time when people can apply the Theory of Change in very concrete ways. They can stop using the services of the predators.
11	Your Plan	Planning Backwards, as taught in Module 6, will help people see the value of that tool and the importance of creating procedural steps. Knowledge and use of the Theory of Change can keep investigators focused on their future story in the midst of chaos; it is the stabilizing factor.

SEQUENCE 3: Relationships During Transition

Explanation: When people begin to make intentional changes in their lives, this inevitably impacts those around them. At the same time, those who surround given individuals can impact them as they begin to work toward their achievement. Some relationships may be lost, and others may be gained.

These phenomena are true for people of all classes, but they're particularly true for people in relationship-based cultures or circumstances. Sometimes the support for change is generally positive, but sometimes it can make transition very difficult. In GA these matters are examined and dealt with directly so that each investigator can be intentional about his/her social capital.

The sequence and reinforcement process begins in Module 1 and is touched on again in Modules 5, 6, 8, 9, and 11.

Module	Content: Mental Models and Activities	Meaning (Explaining the Links) and Tips
1	The activity in which the investigators draw a floor plan of their house or apartment identifies all individuals who sleep in the house or apartment, according to the room in which they sleep. Discuss your thoughts after doing this exercise.	This exercise will establish who is "in your life" in very concrete terms. It will fit into the discussions leading up to the creation of the Mental Model of My Life Now. *Tip:* Don't make the point that some of these people will be taking the journey of change with you, while some may not. The idea that sometimes people have to give up relationships for achievement (at least for a period of time) comes later, in Module 4. This is only to help all group members think concretely about their relationships, to start the sequence.
4	Mental Models of Middle Class and Wealth	When creating the Mental Models of Middle Class and Wealth, the group will be thinking about how stable economic environments might impact relationships in the family and community. *Tip:* Allow the group the time to discuss family and community relationships fully. Again, don't make the point about the potential loss of relationships or the potential for building bridging social capital.
5	Key Points Hidden Rules Family Structure	In the Key Points, give the investigators time to discuss No. 10. Let them make whatever connections they will, to own their own insights, to agree or disagree with the Key Point. In Module 4 group members will develop a mental model of their families that names all the people who have been in it and who are in it now. This is another time that the investigators are putting concrete information on paper. *Tip:* Once the Key Point is "on the table" the facilitator and the investigators can touch base with it as often as it comes up. Every time friends, family, and community are mentioned, this sequence can be brought up.

continued on next page

continued from previous page

Module	Content: Mental Models and Activities	Meaning (Explaining the Links) and Tips
6	Mental Model of Social Capital	After the investigators have created their Mental Model of Social Capital, it would be appropriate to bring up the Key Point again. *Tip:* Whenever it fits into the discovery and discussions of the investigators, give them an "Investigate This" assignment to find where they can build bridging social capital.
8	Self-Assessment of Social Support and Relationships/Role Models	By this time the investigators have had several opportunities to examine their own relationships and will score their resources accordingly.
10	Building Social Support and Relationships/Role Models	This is where the group can investigate the various ways that GA graduates and communities have developed to build social capital.
11	Personal and Community Plans	The Support for Change Mental Model is the final step in this long sequence. It is here that the investigators determine how they will manage their relationships during their transition. *Tip:* It's vital that the investigators make the discoveries about their relationships and decide on their course of action without being directed by the facilitator.

SEQUENCE 4: Motivation

Attending GA doesn't necessarily mean that a person is motivated to get out of poverty, build resources, or use the content in any way. Fortunately, GA is also designed for those who (at least initially) are not motivated; it may be where they find their motivation.

The facilitator's job is to help investigators explore everything about economic class and to trust that most of the investigators will discover and articulate what it is they need to do. There's no sequence for this, even though change is addressed directly throughout the course, particularly in Module 3 (Theory of Change).

Experience shows that there are certain points when investigators begin to express motivation for change. They are:

- Module 1: Directly after determining the debt-to-income ratio or the percentage of income spent on housing. Many people determine right then that they must do something differently, and some begin making changes immediately.

- Module 4: When investigators look into the debt they have accrued because of predatory lenders, some begin to take concrete steps. It takes a long time to get out of debt, but the desire to change is often first articulated then.

- Module 5: The planning activities found in Modules 1, 5, and 6 will grab the attention of some investigators. The Time-Management Matrix in Module 5 is particularly powerful because some people find much of their time going into Quadrants III and IV.

- Module 6: When learning that poverty is about the lack of resources, some people begin to talk about building resources. Doing the Mental Model of Social Capital is another point when individuals start making their own argument for change. They begin to see that they can take steps to form relationships of mutual respect with people in the community.

- Module 8: Many investigators will express their desire to change after they have created the bar chart of personal resources following their self-assessment, if they haven't done so before.

Tip: When it comes to making the argument for change, it should be the voice of the investigator you hear, not your own. The role of the facilitator doesn't include connecting the dots for an investigator or pointing out what resource needs to be built first. Other group members might do that in the course of the discussions; they might challenge one another or even confront each other. But the facilitator, who represents the dominant culture (and who has special status), should resist the urge to tell investigators what to do.

Having issued that caution, it's important to say that there is real joy in hearing investigators express their motivation and take charge of their lives. Facilitators of Getting Ahead report that this tends to be the best part of facilitating the process.

SEQUENCE 5: Relationships with Other Members of the Group and Community

Relationships within the group: Experience shows that the well-established group development process (forming, storming, norming, and performing) usually manifests itself in GA as well, but with added intensity. Module 1 is challenging as the investigators face in very concrete terms the impact that poverty has had on them personally. The relevance of the early modules brings the group members together quickly. The layering of information and the deepening of the dialogue also serve to tighten the bonds of the group. It's common for group members to help each other through a crisis in daily life, to assist each other in study groups, and to share information on how to manage very practical aspects of their lives. After the 16-week workshop has ended, group members often continue to meet informally, and sometimes formally, with or without the support of the sponsoring organization.

Tip: This process is so ingrained in group work that it doesn't require action on the facilitator's part. Members of the group will form in ways to support each other, or they won't. It is theirs to own.

Relationships with community organizations: Investigators from generational poverty whose families may have been involved with service providers and other community institutions are likely to view those organizations with skepticism, even distrust. In Module 1, when building the Mental Model of Poverty, investigators will tell many stories illustrating how that distrust was "earned." Again, in Module 4, when investigators are exploring the causes of poverty in the community and learning how predators work, the sense of anger and distrust can be expected to arise. In Module 4 the group also will likely deepen its understanding of middle class and wealth by creating mental models of those environments. In Module 5 investigators will learn about hidden rules and how that information plays out in community life. In Module 6 the investigators will create a mental model of their own social capital. It's during that exercise that there is sometimes a shift in mindset about organizations. Now, instead of distrusting entire organizations, it's about choosing to trust particular people inside those organizations—people who might become bridging social capital. Later, in Module 9, the group will assess the resource-building capacity of the organizations and determine which organizations, or individuals within them, are worthy of consideration.

Tip: In the early modules when investigators criticize community organizations, don't defend them or offer explanations. It's more important that you listen, that you learn the realities of the investigators, than it is to correct what you think are inaccurate statements. In later modules, when evaluating social capital and organizations, it will be fair to require the objectivity and factual information that may have been missing in the first few sessions.

All of the GA work is based on relationships of mutual respect. Attending to how the group functions together—how relationships are developed in the group and community—is directly tied to future plans, such as keeping a job, picking up an education, and building a balanced life.

Appendix 2
Getting Ahead—the Purpose of Each Module

prepared by Philip DeVol with Kathy McPherson, Lenore Moore, and Tammy Schoonover

Every module has two purposes:

1. **The purpose of the content knowledge of each module.** This knowledge base about poverty is generated by the Getting Ahead investigators themselves as they share their insights into the impact that poverty has on them and their community. They also contribute to the knowledge base by identifying barriers to making the transition out of poverty. The GA investigators also explore the new information found in each module.

2. **The purpose of the learning process that unfolds module by module.** The sequence and reinforcement of the learning experience are intentional. They offer an opportunity for members of the group to learn the change process, articulate their own motivation for change, and build a plan for their personal future story.

In the following chart, the Content Purpose may be shared with the investigators while the Process Purpose is for the facilitator to know.

Module	Content Purpose	Process Purpose
Introduction	Explain the title and history. Explain how the group will work. Establish "ground rules" for the group's self-governance. Establish a comfortable thinking environment.	Interest the potential participant in joining the group. Establish the role of the facilitator as someone who is not superior to the group, but someone with whom the group can work in a co-investigative and synergistic, symbiotic way.
1. My Life upon Release	Define what poverty is like in the community. Identify individual resources: debt-to-income ratio, percentage of income for housing, wage realities. Define what each person's life is like right now.	Establish that the investigators have valuable information that others need to know: for starters, what poverty is like. Establish what life is like now so that investigators can decide throughout the rest of the modules if they want to make changes or not. Establish a feeling of empowerment; encourage participants to see the strength in their own story. Begin the sequence on time management and planning.

continued on next page

continued from previous page

Module	Content Purpose	Process Purpose
2. The Importance of Language	Learn language specific information: registers, discourse patterns, code switching, and story structure. Learn relationship building information: "voices" and the language of negotiation. Learn how to assist children: vocabulary/language experience research, mediation, the penance/forgiveness cycle.	Provide the investigators a safe topic to talk about, a way to practice group rules and experience the role of investigator. Learn how to use language differently, according to the situation. Use language to resolve conflicts and build relationships of mutual respect. Prepare to participate at the planning and decision-making tables. Prepare to help children.
3. Theory of Change (and Stages of Change)	Investigate how to make changes by thinking in the abstract, even when you are in a chaotic situation (the tyranny of the moment). Look/reflect on your life from the outside in (from the abstract to the concrete) rather than from the inside out (from the concrete to the abstract). Move from "I can't because …" to "I can because …" Describe how change takes place so everyone can be aware of his/her own process.	This concept can help free people from the tyranny of the moment. Only some people will get the "tyranny of the moment" idea right away; but if the facilitator reinforces this learning as examples come up during discussions, the entire group will get it by the end. Many goal plans in human services require clients to establish goals/objectives while they are actively in the concrete—while they are often immobilized to see much of anything outside their immediate situation. This type of planning rarely achieves success; clients sign the goal plan out of obligation rather than motivation. Encourage people to be in charge of their own change process. Continue the sequence on planning.

continued on next page

continued from previous page

Module	Content Purpose	Process Purpose
4. The Rich/Poor Gap and Research on Causes of Poverty	Discover that poverty is not caused by just one thing; there are many causes that must be addressed by people at all levels. Establish Mental Models of Middle Class and Wealth.	Connect the concrete experiences of poverty to seemingly abstract information. For example: Connect low wages to how globalization works or how the lack of manufacturing jobs in the community makes it hard for people to get out of poverty. Establish the difference between a stable economic situation (middle class) and a powerful and very stable situation (wealth) and an unstable situation (poverty)—reinforcing the mental models created in Module 1. Deepen understanding of economic class by writing "My Economic Class Story."
5. Hidden Rules of Economic Class	Discover the hidden rules of class. Learn the rules of all classes so that people can navigate the world of work and school more skillfully. Learn the rules in order to develop relationships of mutual respect with others.	Empower people to take a seat at the planning and decision-making tables of institutions and organizations in the community. Continue the sequence on planning.
6. Eleven Resources	Define poverty as the degree to which a person has the 11 resources. It's not just about money; it's about a high-quality, balanced life. Discover the domino effect of resources. Investigate how one issue leads to another—for better or worse	This definition gives people in or near poverty, as well as communities, something to do about poverty: Build resources.
7. Threat Assessment	Focus on patterns of the individual who sabotage their efforts to reenter society successfully. The first 72 hours upon release are when the returning citizen is most vulnerable to old habits.	This assessment and the following assessment of resources are in preparation for making plans.
8. Self-Assessment of Resources	Each investigator establishes his/her individual resources, high and low.	Resources were introduced in Modules 5 and 6. Now the individuals will do an assessment that can show them which resources they need to build. They also will learn what their strongest resources are and how to use high resources to build low resources.

continued on next page

Appendix

continued from previous page

Module	Content Purpose	Process Purpose
9. Community Assessment	Establish the strengths and weaknesses of the community. Share results of the investigation with the community.	Poverty is not just about the mindset or actions of the poor; it's about what is available in the community. Discover assets in the community that can contribute to building resources. Reinforce the value of doing investigations.
10. Building Resources	Learn how to build resources.	This is a natural sequence from the work done in previous modules. This prepares people for the final module.
11. Personal and Community Plans	Develop an individual plan for whatever it is the investigator wants to do. Review SMART goals—define, identify, and practice. Create a one-page mental model that represents the journey that the investigators are making from "what life is like upon release" to the "future story." Create a plan for the community because poverty must be addressed by everyone.	Put old tools and new tools to work. Ideas and concepts are now being put into action. This work is based on the understanding that people in poverty are problem solvers. Many investigators want to help others and their communities. The idea is that GA graduates can join those who plan and run GA and Bridges to continue the work. The information they have about the realities of poverty (created in mental models) and the barriers that people face as they begin to get out of poverty is foundational information for community planners. Some GA graduates will want to join groups that do planning—and participate in creating communities where everyone can live well.
Appendix A of the *Getting Ahead while Getting Out* workbook	Plan the graduation celebration.	This is an end product, but it's really the beginning of new relationships with the facilitator and other group members. The hardest work of GA isn't in doing GA but in supporting people after they're done with GA and are trying to make changes. Bridges and GA organizers must engage the community so that GA graduates get the support they need.

Appendix 3
Model Fidelity Elements for Conducting the Getting Ahead Workshop

prepared by Philip E. DeVol

Thanks to feedback from facilitators and sponsors who use Getting Ahead, we have learned what elements of our model are essential. In order to adhere to our model, sponsors, facilitators, and community collaboratives are asked to ensure the following:

Getting Ahead Model Fidelity Elements	
1. Getting to the table: Getting Ahead graduates are at the planning and decision-making table for all matters that apply to GA.	
2. Diverse poverty experiences: The investigators in each group are from diverse circumstances and backgrounds, most particularly from both situational and generational poverty. This enriches the dialogue and the learning experience.	
3. Sequence and reinforcement: GA is provided in sequence and in the full 20 sessions. There are several learning sequences in GA that allow for reinforcement of difficult concepts. About half of the learning is in the GA content, about half is in the conversations within the group.	
4. Agenda-free: GA investigators choose the resources they want to build, and they pursue the future stories of their own making.	
5. Closed group: GA investigators begin and end the group together. During GA, investigators usually develop a sense of trust that enhances the learning experience and leads to deeper social capital. GA is hard work, and guests and observers would turn GA into a fish bowl that isn't respectful of or helpful to the investigators—so neither is recommended.	
6. Attraction, not coercion: GA investigators are recruited through attraction. Planners are often pushed for quick results and think that forcing people to attend a particular workshop will bring the desired outcome. We know that GA principally attracts people by word of mouth.	
7. Motivation for change: GA investigators make their own arguments for change as a result of the process. Those who participate in the workgroup aren't necessarily expected to be motivated for change at the outset.	
8. Long-term support: Sponsors of GA work with the investigators and the community to create a support system for GA graduates. This includes opportunities to meet regularly, strategies for reducing barriers to transitions, options for building resources, and a variety of pathways out of poverty provided by business, workforce development, education, and other sectors.	
9. Learning community: Provide recordkeeping, data-collection, and quality-improvement activities to improve the GA experience. GA sites are encouraged to learn from and contribute to the Bridges and Getting Ahead Communities of Practice.	

Appendix 4

Activity: Newspapers and Magazines—Understanding How Economic Disparity Affects Us Concretely and Abstractly

Time: 30 minutes
Materials: Chart paper, markers, scissors, tape or glue stick, and daily newspaper or news magazine

1. Investigators separate into two or three groups (depending on size of overall group) by counting off.

2. Each group takes a portion of the periodicals available and finds one article that specifically describes an economic issue that causes disparity and one article that doesn't mention the economy but nonetheless affects communities and causes disparity.

3. Cut out the two articles and paste them to the chart paper and label.

4. Each group chooses a representative to present its findings.

NOTE: This exercise was provided by Mickie Lewis (northeastern Colorado). She said:

> What I found, with this exercise, is that the investigators practiced using their critical voice, sometimes for the first time. I also found that many of the investigators had almost never read newspapers or news periodicals before. One of the quotes I used in my presentation came from this exercise: "I never thought I had the right to talk about this ..." Many individuals deny themselves the right to read, what they consider information above their class. I also found that the investigators starting bringing articles regularly ... some were from magazines ... some newspapers and others from the Internet. We started every session with a sharing time for such things.

Appendix 5
Sustainable Communities Where Everyone Can Live Well

The biggest issue facing our communities—that has yet to hit the radar screen in most places—is the issue of sustainability. The questions our communities must face are:

1. Can we pass on a high quality of life to the next generations?

2. Will everyone, including those on the lower rungs of the economic ladder, be included in "the good life"?

Thomas Sowell (1997), a historical and international researcher, said that none of our towns, cities, or counties can develop a sustainable future if they allow any group to be disenfranchised or left out for any reason (economic class, race, religion, etc.) because the entire community will become economically poorer. Consider poverty, for example. When the percentage of people in poverty reaches 35–40%, the community becomes alarmed, and when it reaches 60%, most of the top 10% move out (Sowell). That's obviously not sustainable. The children left in that community won't be better off if this pattern continues. One can argue that the wealthy children suffer too because they see and encounter little diversity, economic or otherwise.

These political/economic issues and the concept of sustainability are very complex. If we get confused by all the details of complex issues, we can refocus ourselves by coming back to the macro questions:

- How well will future generations of all groups live if this trend continues?

- Will the decisions we are making (whatever they are) create long-term economic stability for all groups now and into the future?

It would seem that creating sustainability is something all economic groups in all countries will have to pay attention to because we're all in this together. For that reason, all three economic groups will need to cooperate and work together.

Here is some information about where the United States ranks in terms of standard, quality-of-life indicators.

Quality-of-life indicators: The United States is one of the 10 wealthiest nations. Even so, quality-of-life issues are a concern. For example, since 1979 inequality in income and wealth (the rich/poor gap) has grown steadily. The divide between the richest families and the poorest is so big that the U.S. ranks third among the 40 most developed countries. The only countries with a bigger divide between the rich and poor are Mexico and Turkey (OECD, Organisation for Economic Cooperation and Development).

The following chart shows data from countries where Bridges and Getting Ahead are being used. It shows the ranking of each country for a number of quality-of-life indicators. The U.S. ranks fourth out of 40 countries, with 17.1% of the people living below 50% of the median income.

OECD Quality-of-Life Indicators for Countries * with Bridges and Getting Ahead Sites	Australia	Canada	Ireland	Slovakia	United Kingdom	United States
Percentage of people living below 50% of median income—about 2005	12.4	11.7	14.8	8.1	8.3	17.1
Rankings in 40 OECD countries						
Percentage of people living below 50% of median income	10	11	5	16	17	4
Educational attainment	22	6	25	2	23	3
Literacy	6	3	17	28	20	14
Subjective well-being	6	2	9	27	14	11
Social network support	6	7	2	25	9	20
Life expectancy	4	10	19	31	22	26
Self-reported health	4	2	5	40	13	3
Working 50-plus hours a week	4	22	25	16	7	7
Time devoted to leisure and personal care	24	25	19	NA	23	23
Percentage votes cast for voting-age population	6	36	21	34	30	31
Percentage votes cast of registered voters	1	34	23	38	32	3
Consultation on rule making	5	4	10	21	1	13
Intentional homicides	24	18	14	17	10	7

Source: Organisation for Economic Cooperation and Development, 2015.

* 40 countries

Discussion

1. What stood out to you from this information about U.S. rankings in the world?

2. What ideas are new to you?

3. How might this information be helpful to you as an individual or helpful to your community?

Appendix 6
Maslow's Hierarchy of Needs

Facilitators are encouraged to share Abraham Maslow's Hierarchy of Needs with investigators in Module 3. It applies not only to the Theory of Change, but it can be utilized when doing the Self-Assessment of Resources in Module 8 and again in Module 10 when making decisions about building resources. Note that the bottom half of Maslow's hierarchy is about getting-by resources, while the top half is about getting-ahead resources.

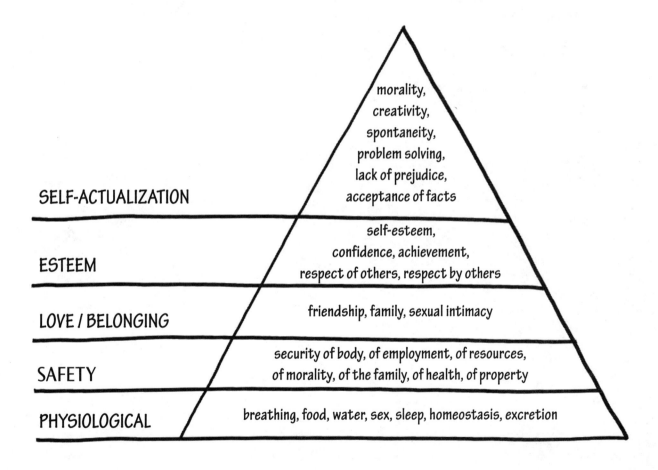

Appendix 7
Data Collection, Evaluations, Research, and Social Capital

Beacon Voice, LLC
www.beaconvoice.com
sam@beaconvoice.com

Charity Tracker, Simon Solutions, Inc.
www.CharityTracker.com
info@charitytracker.com
888-764-0633

Getting Ahead Pre/Post Assessment
St. Joseph County (IN) Bridges Out of Poverty Initiative
www.SJCBridges.org
SJCBridges@gmail.com
574-246-0533

MPOWR, Supply Core, Inc.
www.mpowr.com
brooke.saucier@supplycore.com
815-997-1660

Appendix 8
Websites

aha! Process, Inc: *www.ahaprocess.com*

Bridges™ Out of Poverty: *www.bridgesoutofpoverty.com*

Cascade Engineering: *www.cascadeng.com*

Cincinnati Works: *www.cincinnatiworks.org*

Circles® Campaign: *www.circlescampaign.com*

Community Action Duluth (MN): *www.communityactionduluth.org*

Getting Ahead™ Network: *www.gettingahead.com*

SupplyCore Technology Group: *www.SupplyCore.com/Technology.aspx*

St. Joseph County (IN) Bridges Out of Poverty Initiative: *www.sjcbridges.org*

United for a Fair Economy: *www.faireconomy.org*

Appendix 9
Glossary of Terms Used in Corrections and This *User Guide*

72-Hour Stability Plan: developed in Module 11 and based on work done in Module 7 (Threat Assessment); the 72-Hour Stability plan and the SMART Plan (described below) make up the Getting Ahead Reentry Plan, which is designed to be shared with the Releasing Authority

"Ban the Box": refers to a campaign to remove the "box" from employment application forms asking an applicant whether he/she has ever been convicted of a crime, thereby reducing the impact of hiring decisions based solely on arrest or conviction records

Case management: a collaborative process of assessment, planning, facilitation, care coordination, evaluation, and advocacy for options and services to meet an individual's and family's comprehensive needs through communication and available resources to promote quality, cost-effective outcomes

CBCF (Community-Based Correctional Facility): CBCFs are state-funded correctional facilities and programs that assist local criminal justice systems in reducing prison commitments; a CBCF is a 24-hour secure facility; programs are highly structured with assessment and treatment services to reduce criminal behavior by offenders

Correctional officer: paid staff person responsible for the care, custody, and control of individuals who have been arrested and are awaiting trial or who have been convicted of a crime and sentenced to serve time in a jail or prison

Ex-offender: someone who has previously been convicted of a crime; the term "ex-offender" invites the listener to focus on the word "offender"—the past as opposed to the future—and doesn't aid the rehabilitation process; in Getting Ahead while Getting Out we prefer to use the terms returning citizen, returnee, and/or restored citizen

Felon: a person who has been convicted of a felony, which is a more serious crime than a misdemeanor

Getting Ahead Reentry Plan: developed by investigators in Module 11; this consists of the 72-Hour Stability Plan and the SMART Plan; see "Resources Development Plan" for the other pertinent plan

Halfway house: a center for helping former drug addicts, prisoners, psychiatric patients, or others to adjust to life in general society

Jail: a facility for the confinement of people accused or convicted of a crime, usually on the local level (city or county)

Offender: an individual who commits an illegal act and is prosecuted for it, resulting in a guilty plea or conviction at trial

Prison: a facility in which people are legally held as a punishment for crimes they have committed (or while awaiting trial), usually on a regional or national level (state or federal)

Recidivism: refers to a person's relapse into criminal behavior after he/she receives sanctions or undergoes intervention for a previous crime

Reintegration: restoration to the community, the process of reentry into society

Resources Development Plan: created in Module 11 based on the self-assessment done in Module 8; this is a long-term (approximately three years) plan that is supported by the Getting Ahead Reentry Plan; see 72-Hour Stability Plan and SMART Plan

Restored citizen: reestablishing a person's civil and political rights, which are lost upon conviction; these include the right to run for and hold public office, to serve on a jury, and to work as a notary public; restoration of rights, however, does not include the right to own, possess, or carry a concealed firearm

Returning citizen: an individual who has recently been released from a federal, state, or local correctional facility

SMART (Specific, Measurable, Attainable, Realistic, and Time-specific) Plan: developed in Module 11 and part of the Getting Ahead Reentry Plan; the purpose is to have a detailed approach to all post-release needs— transportation, medication, treatment, housing, employment, etc.

Sober living houses: houses or facilities used by addicts recovering from substance abuse, which serve as an interim environment between rehab and a return to their former lives; sober living environments grew out of a need to have safe and supportive places in which people could live while they were in recovery

Transitional control: a transfer up to 180 days prior to the expiration of a prison term or release on parole, under closely monitored supervision and confinement in the community, such as a stay in a licensed halfway house or restriction to an approved residence on electronic monitoring, usually approved by the committing county judge

Treatment "in lieu of": allows for a court to permit a criminal defendant facing a specific charge to receive treatment instead of facing a trial and possible conviction and incarceration; usually an option only for first-time offenders; "in lieu of" means "instead of"

NOTES

Bibliography

Akerlof, G. A., & Kranton, R. E. (2010). *Identity economics: How our identities shape our work, wages, and well-being.* Princeton, NJ: Princeton University Press.

Albelda, R., Folbre, N., & Center for Popular Economics. (1996). *The war on the poor: A defense manual.* New York, NY: The New Press.

Alexander, Michelle. (2010). *The new Jim Crow: Mass incarceration in the age of colorblindness.* New York, NY: The New Press.

Alexie, S. (2007). *The absolutely true diary of a part-time Indian.* New York, NY: Little, Brown.

Andreas, S., & Faulkner, C. (Eds.). (1994). NLP: *The new technology of achievement.* New York, NY: Quill.

Anzaldúa, G. (2007). *Borderlands la frontera: The new mestiza* (3rd ed.). San Francisco, CA: Aunt Lute Books.

Barkai, J. (1996). Teaching negotiation and ADR: The savvy samurai meets the devil. *Nebraska Law Review, 75,* 704–751.

Becker, K. A., Krodel, K. M., & Tucker, B. H. (2009). *Understanding and engaging under-resourced college students: A fresh look at the influence of economic class on teaching and learning in higher education.* Highlands, TX: aha! Process.

Biggs, J. B. (1986). Enhancing learning skills: The role of metacognition. In J. A. Bowden (Ed.), Student learning: *Research into practice* (pp. 131–148). Melbourne, Australia: University of Melbourne Press.

Block, P. (2009). *Community: The structure of belonging.* San Francisco, CA: Berrett-Koehler.

Brookfield, S. D. (1990). *The skillful teacher: On technique, trust, and responsiveness in the classroom.* San Francisco, CA: Jossey-Bass.

Brouwer, S. (1998). *Sharing the pie: A citizen's guide to wealth and power in America.* New York, NY: Henry Holt.

Brown, J. S., Collins, A., & Duguid, P. (1989). Situated cognition and the culture of learning. *Educational Researcher, 18*(1), 32–42.

Burd-Sharps, S., Lewis, K., & Martins, E. B. (2008). *The measure of America: American human development report 2008–2009.* New York, NY: Columbia University Press.

Chapman, K. J. (2001). Measuring intent: There's nothing 'mere' about mere measurement effects. *Psychology and Marketing, 18*(8), 811–841.

Chinni, D., & Gimpel, J. (2010). *Our patchwork nation: The surprising truth about the 'real' America.* New York, NY: Penguin Group.

Coles, W. E. (1992, November). Keynote address. Paper presented at Composition Coordinators' Retreat, Kent State University Regional Campus System, Newbury, OH.

Covey, S. R. (1989). *The 7 habits of highly effective people: Powerful lessons in personal change.* New York, NY: Simon & Schuster.

Crum, T. F. (1998). *The magic of conflict: Turning a life of work into a work of art.* New York, NY: Simon & Schuster.

Daniels, C. (2007). *Ghettonation: A journey into the land of bling and the home of the shameless.* New York, NY: Doubleday.

Davidson, R. J., & Begley, S. (2012). *The emotional life of your brain: How its unique patterns affect the way you think, feel, and live—and how you can change them.* New York, NY: Hudson Street Press.

DeParle, J. (2004). *American dream: Three women, ten kids, and a nation's drive to end welfare.* New York, NY: Viking Penguin.

de Soto, H. (2000). *The mystery of capital: Why capitalism triumphs in the West and fails everywhere else.* New York, NY: Basic Books.

DeVol, P. E. (2010). *Bridges to sustainable communities: A systemwide, cradle-to-grave approach to ending poverty in America.* Highlands, TX: aha! Process.

DeVol, P. E., & Krodel, K. M. (2010). *Facilitator notes for investigations into economic class in America.* Highlands, TX: aha! Process.

DeVol, P. E., & Krodel, K. M. (2010). *Investigations into economic class in America.* Highlands, TX: aha! Process.

DiClemente, C. C., & Velasquez, M. M. (2002). Motivational interviewing and the stages of change. In W. R. Miller & S. Rollnick (Eds.), *Motivational interviewing: Preparing people for change* (2nd ed., pp. 201–216). New York, NY: Guilford Press.

Diller, Jerry V. (1999). *Cultural diversity: A primer for the human services.* Belmont, CA: Wadsworth Publishing Company.

Donnelly, J. (Ed.). (1997). *Who are the question-makers? A participatory evaluation handbook.* New York, NY: Office of Evaluation and Strategic Planning, United Nations Development Program.

Doran, G. T. (1981). There's a S.M.A.R.T. way to write management's goals and objectives. *Management Review, 70*(11), 35–36.

Dowst, K. (1980). The epistemic approach: Writing, knowing, and learning. In T. R. Donovan & B. W. McClelland (Eds.), *Eight approaches to teaching composition* (pp. 65–85). Urbana, IL: National Council of Teachers of English.

Drill down. (2010). Retrieved from *http://www.mindtools.com/pages/article/newTMC_02.htm*

Fairbanks, M. (2000). Changing the mind of a nation: Elements in a process for creating prosperity. In L. E. Harrison & S. P. Huntington (Eds.), *Culture matters: How values shape human progress* (pp. 268–281). New York, NY: Basic Books.

Farson, R. (1997). *Management of the absurd: Paradoxes in leadership.* New York, NY: Touchstone.

Feuerstein, R. (1985). Structural cognitive modifiability and Native Americans. In S. Unger (Ed.), To sing our own songs: *Cognition and culture in Indian education* (pp. 21–36). New York, NY: Association on American Indian Affairs.

Fisher, R., & Ury, W. (1983). *Getting to YES: Negotiating agreement without giving in.* New York, NY: Penguin.

Freedman, J., & Combs, G. (1996). *Narrative therapy: The social construction of preferred realities.* New York, NY: Norton.

Friedman, B. M. (2006). *The moral consequences of economic growth.* New York, NY: Vintage Books.

Freire, P. (1999). *Pedagogy of the oppressed.* New York, NY: Continuum.

Fuller, R. W. (2004). *Somebodies and nobodies: Overcoming the abuse of rank.* Gabriola Island, BC: New Society Publishers.

Fussell, P. (1983). *Class: A guide through the American status system.* New York, NY: Touchstone.

Galbraith, J. K. (2008). *The predator state: How conservatives abandoned the free market and why liberals should too.* New York, NY: Free Press.

Galeano, E. (1998). *Upside down: A primer for the looking-glass world.* New York, NY: Metropolitan Books.

Gans, H. J. (1995). The war against the poor. New York, NY: Basic Books.

Gee, J. P. (1987). What is literacy? Teaching and learning: *The Journal of Natural Inquiry, 2*(1), 3–11.

Glasmeier, A. K. (2006). *An atlas of poverty in America: One nation, pulling apart, 1960–2003.* New York, NY: Routledge.

Goleman, D. (1995). *Emotional intelligence.* New York, NY: Bantam Books.

Goleman, D. (2006). *Social intelligence: The new science of human relationships.* New York. NY: Bantam.

The growing divide: Inequality and the roots of economic insecurity trainer's manual. (2009). Boston, MA: United for a Fair Economy.

Haque, U. (2011). *The new capitalist manifesto: Building a disruptively better business.* Boston, MA: Harvard Business Review Press.

Harrison, L. E., & Huntington, S. P. (Eds.). (2000). *Culture matters: How values shape human progress.* New York, NY: Basic Books.

Hart, B., & Risley, T. R. (1995). *Meaningful differences in the everyday experience of young American children.* Baltimore, MD: Paul H. Brookes.

Henderson, N. (1996). *Resiliency in schools: Making it happen for students and educators.* Thousand Oaks, CA: Corwin Press.

hooks, bell. (2000). *Where we stand: Class matters.* New York, NY: Routledge.

Horstman, M. (n.d.). How to give feedback. Retrieved from *http://www.manager-tools.com/podcasts/Manager_Tools_Feedback_Model.pdf*

Jaworski, J. (1996). *Synchronicity: The inner path of leadership.* San Francisco, CA: Berrett-Koehler.

Jenkins, L. (2004). *Permission to forget: And nine other root causes of America's frustration with education.* Milwaukee, WI: ASQ Quality Press.

Johnson, A. G. (2006). *Privilege, power, and difference* (2nd ed.). New York, NY: McGraw-Hill.

Joos, M. (1967). The styles of the five clocks. In R. D. Abraham & R. C. Troike (Eds.), *Language and cultural diversity in American education* (pp. 145–149). Englewood Cliffs, NJ: Prentice Hall.

Kelly, M. (2001). *The divine right of capital: Dethroning the corporate aristocracy.* San Francisco, CA: Berrett-Koehler.

Kelly, T. L. (2004). The theme of transformation in the work of Carl Upchurch. *The new tomorrow: A voice for blacks and Latinos.* Retrieved from http://web.pdx.edu/~psu17799/upchurch.htm

Kimmel, M. S., & Ferber, A. L. (Eds.). (2010). *Privilege: A reader.* Boulder, CO: Westview Press.

Kiyosaki, R. T., & Lechter, S. L. (1998). *Rich dad, poor dad.* Paradise Valley, AZ: TechPress.

Klein, N. (2007). *The shock doctrine: The rise of disaster capitalism.* New York, NY: Metropolitan Books.

Kretzmann, J. P., & McKnight, J. L. (1993). *Building communities from the inside out: A path toward finding and mobilizing a community's assets.* Chicago, IL: ACTA.

Kretzmann, J. P., & McKnight, J. L. (with Dobrowolski, S., & Puntenney, D.). (2005). *Discovering community power: A guide to mobilizing local assets and your organization's capacity.* Evanston, IL: Asset-Based Community Development Institute. Retrieved from http://www.abcdinstitute.org/docs/kelloggabcd.pdf

Krodel, K., Becker, K., Ingle, H., & Jakes, S. (2008). *Helping under-resourced learners succeed at the college and university level: What works, what doesn't, and why.* Retrieved from http://www.ahaprocess.com

Lareau, A. (2003). *Unequal childhoods: Class, race, and family life.* Berkeley, CA: University of California Press.

Lave, J., & Wenger, E. (1991). *Situated learning: Legitimate peripheral participation.* New York, NY: Cambridge University Press.

Leondar-Wright, B. (2005). *Class matters: Cross-class alliance building for middle-class activists.* Gabriola Island, Canada: New Society Publishers.

Lind, M. (2004). Are we still a middle-class nation? *The Atlantic, 293*(1), 120–128. Retrieved from http://www.ahaprocess.com/files/HelpingURLSucceed_whitepaper05152009.pdf

Lobovits, D., & Prowell, J. (1996). Unexpected journey: Invitations to diversity. Retrieved from http://www.narrativeapproaches.com/narrative%20papers%20folder/journey_chart.htm

Lopez, L. M. (Ed.). (2009). *An angle of vision: Women writers on their poor and working-class roots.* Ann Arbor, MI: University of Michigan Press.

Lui, M., Robles, B., Leondar-Wright, B., Brewer, R., & Adamson, R. (2006). *The color of wealth: The story behind the U.S. racial wealth divide.* New York, NY: The New Press.

Lupton, R. D. (2011). *Toxic charity: How churches and charities hurt those they help (and how to reverse it).* New York, NY: HarperCollins.

Marzano, R. J. (2007). *The art and science of teaching: A comprehensive framework for effective instruction.* Alexandria, VA: Association for Supervision and Curriculum Development.

Martinot, S. (2003). *The rule of racialization: Class, identity, governance.* Philadelphia, PA: Temple University Press.

McKnight, J. (1995). *The careless society: Community and its counterfeits.* New York, NY: Basic Books.

Mehrabian, A. (1981). *Silent messages: Implicit communications of emotions and attitudes.* Belmont, CA: Wadsworth.

MGTC24: Detailed outline of weekly activities. (n.d.). Retrieved from *http://www.utsc.utoronto. ca/~phanira/WebSkills/fall09-course-outline-skills.htm*

Michaels, W. B. (2006). *The trouble with diversity: How we learned to love identity and ignore inequality.* New York, NY: Metropolitan Books.

Miller, M. (2009). *The tyranny of dead ideas: Letting go of the old ways of thinking to unleash a new prosperity.* New York, NY: Times Books.

Miller, W. R., & Rollnick, S. (2002). *Motivational interviewing: Preparing people for change* (2nd ed.). New York, NY: Guilford Press.

Miringoff, M., & Miringoff, M.-L. (1999). *The social health of the nation: How America is really doing.* New York, NY: Oxford University Press.

Montano-Harmon, M. R. (1991). Discourse features of written Mexican Spanish: Current research in contrastive rhetoric and its implications. *Hispania, 74*(2), 417–425.

Moustakas, C. E. (1966). *The authentic teacher: Sensitivity and awareness in the classroom.* Cambridge, MA: Howard A. Doyle.

Murray, C. (2012). Coming apart: The state of white America, 1960–2010. New York, NY: Crown Forum.

National College Transition Network. (2009). College for adults. Retrieved from *http://www.collegeforadults.org*

O'Connor, A. (2001). *Poverty knowledge: Social science, social policy, and the poor in twentieth-century U.S. history.* Princeton, NJ: Princeton University Press.

Palmer, P. J. (1998). *The courage to teach: Exploring the inner landscape of a teacher's life.* San Francisco, CA: Jossey-Bass.

Payne, R. K. (2008). *Under-resourced learners: 8 strategies to boost student achievement.* Highlands, TX: aha! Process.

Payne, R. K. (2012). *A framework for understanding poverty: 10 actions to educate students.* Highlands, TX: aha! Process.

Payne, R. K. (2013). *A framework for understanding poverty: A cognitive approach* (5th rev. ed.). Highlands, TX: aha! Process.

Payne, R. K., DeVol, P. E., & Smith, T. D. (2009). *Bridges out of poverty: Strategies for professionals and communities* (4th rev. ed.). Highlands, TX: aha! Process.

Pfarr, J. R. (2009). *Tactical communication: Law enforcement tools for successful encounters with people from poverty, middle class, and wealth.* Highlands, TX: aha! Process.

Phillips, K. (2002). *Wealth and democracy: A political history of the American rich.* New York, NY: Broadway Books.

Pimpare, S. (2008). *A people's history of poverty in America.* New York, NY: The New Press.

Pransky, J. (1998). *Modello: A story of hope for the inner city and beyond.* Cabot, VT: Northeast Health Realization Institute.

Putnam, R. D. (2000). *Bowling alone: The collapse and revival of American community.* New York, NY: Simon & Schuster.

Rivlin, G. (2010). Broke, USA: *From pawnshops to Poverty, Inc.—How the working poor became big business.* New York, NY: HarperCollins.

Robinson, E. (2010). *Disintegration: The splintering of black America.* New York, NY: Doubleday.

Rose, M. (1989). *Lives on the boundary: The struggles and achievements of America's underprepared.* New York, NY: Free Press.

Roseland, M. (2005). *Toward sustainable communities: Resources for citizens and their governments.* Gabriola Island, Canada: New Society Publishers.

Rothenberg, P. S. (2005). *White privilege: Essential readings on the other side of racism* (2nd ed.). New York, NY: Worth Publishers.

Sapolsky, R. M. (1998). *Why zebras don't get ulcers: An updated guide to stress, stress-related diseases, and coping.* New York, NY: W. H. Freeman.

Sawyer, D. (Anchor). (1991). True colors [Television series episode segment]. In M. Lukasiewicz (Producer), *PrimeTime Live.* New York, NY: American Broadcasting Corporation.

Schwartz, P. (1996). *The art of the long view.* New York, NY: Currency Doubleday.

Senge, P. M. (1990). *The fifth discipline: The art and practice of the learning organization.* New York, NY: Currency Doubleday.

Senge, P., Smith, B., Kruschwitz, N., Laur, J., & Schley, S. (2010). *The necessary revolution: Working together to create a sustainable world.* New York, NY: Broadway Books.

Sharron, H., & Coulter, M. (2004). *Changing children's minds: Feuerstein's revolution in the teaching of intelligence.* Highlands, TX: aha! Process.

Shaughnessy, M. P. (1977). *Errors and expectations: A guide for the teacher of basic writing.* New York, NY: Oxford University Press.

Shebat, G. (2009). *Fundamentals of college writing* [Course assignments]. Youngstown, OH: Youngstown State University.

Shipler, D. K. (2004). *The working poor: Invisible in America.* New York, NY: Alfred A. Knopf.

Shuman, M. H. (2007). *The small-mart revolution: How local businesses are beating the global competition.* San Francisco, CA: Berrett-Koehler.

Smith, A. (1994). *An inquiry into the nature and causes of the wealth of nations.* New York, NY: The Modern Library.

Smith, L. (2010). *Psychology, poverty, and the end of social exclusion: Putting our practice to work.* New York, NY: Teachers College Press.

Smith, H. (1994). *The illustrated world's religions: A guide to our wisdom traditions.* New York, NY: HarperCollins.

Sowell, T. (1997). *Migrations and cultures: A world view.* New York, NY: HarperCollins.

Sowell, T. (1998, October 5). Race, culture, and equality. *Forbes,* 144–149.

"Special report: CEO compensation." (2008, April 30). Forbes. Retrieved from *http://www.forbes.com/lists/2008/12/lead_bestbosses08_CEO-Compensation_Rank.html*

Stout, L. (2011). *Collective visioning: How groups can work together for a just and sustainable future.* San Francisco, CA: Berrett-Koehler.

Surowiecki, J. (2005). *The wisdom of crowds.* New York, NY: Anchor.

Taylor-Ide, D., & Taylor, C. E. (2002). *Just and lasting change: When communities own their futures.* Baltimore, MD: Johns Hopkins University Press.

Tett, G. (2010). Fool's gold: *The inside story of J. P. Morgan and how Wall Street greed corrupted its bold dream and created a financial catastrophe.* New York, NY: Free Press.

Twin Cities RISE! (2009). *Empowerment: A course in personal empowerment.* Minneapolis; MN: Author. Tuckman, B. W. (1965). Developmental sequence in small groups. *Psychological Bulletin, 63*(6), 384–399.

Upchurch, C. (1996). *Convicted in the womb.* New York, NY: Bantam Books.

Valenzuela, C., & Addington, J. (2006a). *Four features of racism* [Available from Minnesota Collaborative Anti-Racism Initiative, 1671 Summit Ave., St. Paul, MN 55105].

Valenzuela, C., & Addington, J. (2006b). *Systemic racism: Daily strategies for survival and beyond* [Available from Minnesota Collaborative Anti-Racism Initiative, 1671 Summit Ave., St. Paul, MN 55105].

Vella, J. (2002). *Learning to listen, learning to teach: The power of dialogue in educating adults* (rev. ed.). San Francisco, CA: Jossey-Bass.

Washburne, C. (1958). Conflicts between educational theory and structure. *Educational Theory, 8*(2), 87–94.

Wenger, E., McDermott, R., & Snyder, W. M. (2002). *Cultivating communities of practice: A guide to managing knowledge.* Boston, MA. Harvard Business School Publishing.

WETA. (2010). Home. *Retrieved from http://www.ldonline.org/index.php*

Wheeler, R. S. (2008). Becoming adept at code-switching. *Educational Leadership, 65*(7), 54–58.

Wheeler, R. S., & Swords, R. (2006). *Code-switching: Teaching Standard English in urban classrooms.* Urbana, IL: National Council of Teachers of English.

Wheeler, R. S., & Swords, R. (2010). *Code-switching lessons: Grammar strategies for linguistically diverse writers.* Portsmouth, NH: Heinemann.

Wilkinson, R. G., & Pickett, K. (2009). *The spirit level: Why more equal societies almost always do better.* London, England: Penguin.

Wilson, W. J. (1990). The truly disadvantaged: The inner city, the underclass, and public policy. Chicago, IL: The University of Chicago Press.

World Bank. (2005). *World development report 2006: Equity and development.* New York, NY: Oxford University Press.

Zull, J. (2002). *The art of changing the brain: Enriching the practice of teaching by exploring the biology of learning.* Sterling, VA: Stylus.

Index

NOTE: Page numbers in *italics* refer to display text or illustrations.

A

Abstract thinking
    benefits of, 3
    challenges for investigators in moving to, 13
    economic class and, 103
    in Getting Ahead philosophy, 9
    in investigation of Theory of Change Mental Model, 85, *86–87*
    mediation to promote, 87
    mental models and, 4, 9, 87
    poverty as obstacle to, 2
    social capital and capacity for, 87
    strategies for shifting from concrete thinking to, 87
Accountability
    charts, 17, *18, 22*
    for Getting Ahead classes, 17, *18*
    in Getting Ahead Model, 16, 17
    for Getting Out initiative, 17, *22*
    meaning of, 16
Agenda-free approach, 3, 5, 6, 14, 34–35, 56, *155*
aha! Process, Inc., 24, 45, 65, 161
Art of the Long View, The (Schwartz), 85

B

Ban the Box, 162
Bates, B., *44*
Baum, D., 10
Bazata, B., 33
Beacon Voice, LLC, 160
Bonding Capital, 109
Bowling Alone (Putnam), 42
Bridges Collaboratives, 22
    in implementation of Getting Ahead in correctional institutions, 16
    organizing, x
    participants in, 24
    participation of Getting Ahead graduates in, 21
    problem-solving approach of, 57
    resources for, 24
    role of, ix
    role of, in reentry program, ix, x, 26, 57

Bridges Communities, support for Reentry Model from, ix, 22, 23, 33
Bridges Constructs, 23
    training in, 25
Bridges Continuum, 35, *36–37*
Bridges initiatives
    community models, 44
    Getting Ahead and, 25, 26, 33
    structure and operations, *39–40*
    support for graduates of. *See* Support for graduates of Bridges and Getting Ahead programs
    unique features of, 33
    websites, 44
Bridges Institutes, 40
Bridges Out of Poverty, ix, 2, 22, 24, 25, 45
Bridges™ Out of Poverty, 161
Bridges Steering Committees
    comprehensive strategies for, in Bridges Continuum, *36–37*
    support for Getting Ahead graduates from, 42
Bridges to Sustainable Communities, 24, 25
Bridging social capital. *See* Social capital
Brookfield, S., 63

C

Carr, F., 111
Cascade Engineering, 45, 161
Case management
    cloud-based evaluation tools, 28, *30*
    defined, 162
    web-based community collaboration tools, *32*
CEO Pay Gap Activity, 98–99
Change
    asking questions to facilitate, 9
    challenges for investigators, 13, 89
    counselor's role in facilitating, 13, 149
    in Getting Ahead philosophy, 3
    in identity, *43*
    motivation for, 13, 58, 149
    relationships and, 109, *147–148*
    Stages of, 60, 89, *89*

in use of time, 43
  See also Module 3, Theory of Change
Charity Tracker, 28, *30,* 125, 160
Children, 11, 24, 37, 77, 79, *79,* 80
Choice, 16
Cincinnati Works, 45
Circles® Campaign, 161
Circles of Support, 34, 42
Circular story pattern, 69
Cloud-based evaluation tools, 28, *30*
Code switching, 11, *78, 152*
Co-facilitators
  role of, 15, 63
  sources of, 15
  working with former investigators as, 63
Cognitive dissonance, *7,* 85, 89
Co-investigation
  authentic relationship in, 14
  defined, 1
  in Getting Ahead philosophy, 6, 7
  mutual respect in, 3
College Achievement Alliance, 45, *46*
Combs, G., 9
Community assessment. *See* Module 10, Community Assessment
Community-based correctional facility, 4, 162
Community Prosperity, Mental Model of, 9, *139*
Community resources assessment, 3. *See also* Module 10, Community Assessment
Community story, *6,* 8
Community support, *40–41*
Community sustainability
  Facilitators' and sponsors' understanding of, 1
  importance of, 157
  quality-of-life indicators, 157–158
  threats to, 157
Community Sustainability Grid, *105*
Community volunteers, 26, 27
Concrete thinking
  as core construct, 9
  economic class and, 103
  in investigation of Theory of Change Mental Model, 85, 86–87
  in poverty, 3
  strategies for shifting to abstract thinking from, 87
Corporate and business sector, 45
Correctional institutions
  hidden rules of, 56
  using Getting Ahead in, 16, 26
  working with offenders in, 56–57

Corrections staff
  in implementation of Reentry Model, 25, 26
  officers, 162
  resources for, 24
  role in recruiting investigators, 19
  working with, 57
Countrywide Financial, 99
Courts and criminal justice system, 47
Crimogenic Needs, 28
Critical analysis, 3, 11
Culture of learning, 11, *12*

D

Data collection
  on program effectiveness, 23, 28, *29*
  for program success, x
  rationale, 28
  resources, 160
  tools, 28–32
de Souza Briggs, X., *45*
Detachment, *86,* 87
DeVol, P., ix, 9
Discovering Patterns in My Life, *122*
Discrepancy-making process, *7,* 13, 85, 89
Dixon Correctional Facility, Baton Rouge (LA), 47
Dominated and dominant groups, 13–15, 55
Drucker, P., 99
Drug courts, 34, 47
Duluth (MN) Community Action, 161
Duluth (MN) Community Engagement Strategy, 44

E

Education
  defined, 11
  goals of, 2
  postsecondary, support for Getting Ahead graduates in, 45
Eisenhower Foundation, 27
Emerald, D., 57
Employee assistance programs, 45
Ex-offender, 57, 162
Expectations, 17, 64
Exploitation, 93

F

Facilitators
  in change process, 13, 149
  in co-investigation, 1, 3, 7, 14
  in development of group mental models, 10

dominant culture status of, 13–15, 55
in exploration of language and vocabulary, 11
good qualities of, 53
group management strategies, 58, 60–64
group meeting attendance requirements for, 20
in "kitchen table" learning, 4–5
listening skills of, 7
number of, in Getting Ahead sessions, 5
preparation for implementing Reentry Model, x
questioning techniques, 61–62
in recruitment of investigators, 19
relationships with investigators, 58, 63–64
role of, 16, 53, 70
self-evaluation, 55
sequential implementation of Getting Ahead by, 8
sources of, 5
support for, 20, 64–65, 67
training and certification, x, 5, 20, 24, 25, 26–27
trusting in process, 15
using *Getting Out* workbook, 54
working in correctional facilities, 56–57
working with correctional staff, 57
working with returning citizens, 57
False generosity, 14
Families of incarcerated and returning citizens
creating mental model of, *113*
investigating issues around, *113, 114*
in Reentry Model, x, 26
resources for, 24
Farson, R., 13, *58*
Federal Poverty Guidelines, 117
Felon, 162
Financing, 51
Food stamps, 48, 49
Ford, Henry, 26
Foster care programs, 34
Foundations, 51
Framework for Understanding Poverty, A (Payne), 45
Franklin County (OH) Drug Court, 47
Freedman, J., 9
Freire, P., 13
Frequently asked questions, 25–28
Funders, 51
preparation for implementing Reentry Model, x
resources for implementing Reentry Model, 24

Fundraising, 21
Future stories, 39
goals of Getting Ahead, 2, 3, 34
module sequence for investigation of, 145–146
Future Story Portfolio, *138, 139*
contents, *75, 81, 84, 105, 108, 115, 118, 124, 130, 134, 138, 139*

G

Getting Ahead in a Just-Gettin'-By World, ix, 1, 22, 24
Getting Ahead Mobile App, *31*
Getting Ahead model and initiatives
accountability in, 16, 17, 18
as agenda-free, 3, 5, 6, 14, 34–35, 56, *155*
Bridges initiatives and, 23, 33, 35
budget items, 19
causes of poverty in, 2, 91
conceptualization of resources in, 49–51
fidelity elements, 21, 155
incomes of participating investigators, 117
Learning Experience, *6–7*
philosophical basis of, 1, 2–4, 7
as power-based approach, 49
program performance assessments, *28, 29, 30*
sequence of implementation, 8
settings for implementation, 34
sponsoring organizations, 33–34
support for graduates of programs. *See* Support for graduates of Bridges and Getting Ahead programs
support from aha! Process for, 35
underlying sequences of, 70
unique features of, 6, 66
websites, 44, 65
Getting Ahead Network, 64–65, 161
Getting Ahead while Getting Out, ix, x
in correctional institutions, 16
user guides, 19
workbook, 19, 24, 54
See also Reentry Model
Getting Out initiatives
accountability chart, 17, *22*
budget for, 19
coordination between, 21
fundraising for, 21
media coverage for, 21
recordkeeping, 21

recruiting for, 19
  See also Reentry Model
Getting Out Learning Community, 24
Graduates, Bridges. *See* Support for graduates of Bridges and Getting Ahead programs
Graduation of Getting Ahead investigators, 140, 154. *See also* Support for graduates of Bridges and Getting Ahead programs
Groups
- accountability in, 16, 17
- co-facilitator role in, 15
- commenting on work of, 61
- continuum of environmental stability of members of, *5*
- creating mental models in, 10, 60–61
- emotional issues in, 62
- feeling of safety in, 7
- introducing new information in, 69–70
- in "kitchen table" learning experience, 4–5
- make-up sessions, 58
- managing discussions in, 58, 60, 69
- meeting schedule, 20, 58, *59*
- orientation for, 19–20
- ownership of, 69
- phases of development of, 9, 150
- potential problems in, 62
- preparing for closure, 63
- pre/post assessment and feedback, 28, *29*
- recruiting, 19
- relationships among members of, 150
- rituals for, 60, 69
- rules for, 7, 62, 71
- settings for meetings, 4, 5, 7, 20
- size of, ix, 5
- start of session, 60, 69
- supplies for, 20
- troubleshooting problems in, 20

Gruza, M., *140*
Guiding Coalitions, 42

H

Halfway houses, 26, 48, 162
Hart, B., 80
Health and wellness, 35
Hidden rule for time, 111–112
Hidden rules of economic class, 2, 9
- conflict over, 113
- defined, 3
- knowledge of, as power, 111
- module sequence for investigation of, *143–144*
- resources and, 111
- self-perception and, 112
- taking responsibility for, 113
- use of, 3
- value of understanding, 107, 112
- *See also* Module 5, Hidden Rules of Economic Class

Hidden rules of incarceration, *110*
Hidden rules of prison life, 56
Hierarchy of Needs, 89, 159
Hospitals and healthcare settings, 45, 47

I

Incarceration
- hidden rules of, *110*
- investigating causes of, 92

Income distribution and disparity, 157
- exercises and activities for exploring, *75, 95,* 96–101, 156
- module sequence for investigation of, *143–144*

Income Quintiles Activity, 96–97
Income vs. wealth, 100–101
Institutional and community resources, poverty effects on, 4
Interviews, 129
Investigations into Economic Class in America, 11, 35, 45
Investigators
- accountability in groups, 16
- in co-investigation, 7
- commenting on work of, in groups, 61
- context for learning, 2
- distrust of agencies and service providers, 13, 150
- facilitators' relationship with, 58, 63–64
- graduation, 140
- in "kitchen table" learning experience, 4–5
- literacy skills, 10
- orientation for, 19–20
- recruiting, 19
- role of, 15, 16, 70
- using *Getting Out* workbook, 54
- working in correctional settings with, 56–57
- *See also* Groups; Support for graduates of Bridges and Getting Ahead programs

J

Jail, 26, 162
Jaworski, J., 10
Just and Lasting Change: When Communities Own Their Futures (Taylor-Ide & Taylor), *48*

K

Kent State University, 47
"Kitchen table" learning, 4–5, 135
Kiyosaki, R., 111
Krodel, K., 11

L

Language
    in child development, 79, 80
    code switching, *78*
    of conflict, *81*
    of *Getting Out* workbook, 54
    goals of Getting Ahead, 11
    Module 2 investigations into, *78*
    of negotiation, 81, *81*
    of questioning techniques, 61
    registers of, 7, 11, 53, 54, 62, 64, 78, 111
    three voices, *78*
    See also Module 2, The Importance of Language
Lareau, A., 80
Learning
    changing thinking from situated cognition to culture of, 11, *12*
    from content and from discussion, *6*, 7
    continuous, in Getting Ahead, 56
    "kitchen table," 4–5, 135
    life as context for, 2, *6*
    mental models and, 10
    within modules, 70
    Process Triangle, 8, 54, 71
    reinforcement in, 8, 142
    relational, 63
    sequence, 8, 142
    unique features of Getting Ahead, *6–7*
    workbook objectives, 54
Learning communities, x, 20, 21, 23, 24, 40, 41, 42, 56, 64, *155*
Learning to Listen, Learning to Teach (Vella), 8, 58
Left-handed conversations, 60
Levine, M., 80
Lewis, M., *15*
Libster, Mitchell, ix

Listening, 7, 62
Literacy, 10
Lobovits, D., 13–15
Longview (TX) Bridges Buddies, 42

M

Mackey, J., 99
Make-up sessions, 58
Management of the Absurd (Farson), 13, *58*
Marzano, R., 63
Maslow, A., 159
Maslow's Hierarchy of Needs, 89, 159
Meals, 4, 20
Meaningful Differences in the Everyday Experience of Young American Children (Hart & Risley), 80
Media coverage, 21
Mediation, *79*, 87, 133
Mediation chart, 54
Medicaid, 48
Meeting space, 4, 5, 7, 20
Mental health issues, 62
Mental model(s)
    awareness of, 10
    community assessment, 127, *128*, 129
    of Community Prosperity, 9, *139*
    creating, in Getting Ahead groups, 60–61
    defined, 9
    of Floor Plan of Apartment/House Where I Will Live upon My Release, *75*
    in Getting Ahead philosophy, 2, 9
    in *Getting Out* workbook, 54
    group processes in creation of, 10
    introducing concept of, 72
    of middle class and wealth, *102*, 103–104, 111, 143, 150, *153*
    of My Family Structure, *113*
    of My Future Story, *139*, 140
    of My Life upon Release, 73, 89, 140
    One-on-One Relationships, 127, *130*, 131
    personal, 61
    of poverty, 9, 10, *72*, *73*, 73–74, 129
    of process of change, 85–87, *88*
    to promote abstract thinking, 9, 87
    purpose of, 3, 4, *7*, 9–10, 10
    of resources, *124*
    of social capital, *118*, 150
    Support for Change, *139*
    use of, for educational and publicity purposes, 61
Metacognition, 83, 85

Middle class
- benefits of Getting Ahead for, 2, 41
- capacity for abstract thinking and future focus, 9, 13
- creation of, *95*
- current state of, 14
- facilitator's status as, 55
- in Getting Ahead partnerships, 4, 44, 67, 131
- hidden rules of, 111, 112
- investigation into creation of, *95*
- linkage with poor, 14
- mental model of, 102, 103–104, 111, 143, 150, *153*
- "righting reflex," 33

Miller, E., *10*
Miller, W., *13*
Mind at a Time, A (Levine), 80
Model Fidelity, x
- checklist, 21
- Getting Ahead elements, 155

Module 1, My Life upon Release, 7
- agenda, *72, 75*
- closing, *75*
- content and process purposes of, *151*
- facilitator role, *72, 75*
- investigator role, *72, 75*
- learning process, *72, 75*
- mental model investigations in, *13,* 73–74, 89
- session goals, 71, *75*
- session preparation, 71
- *See also* Modules

Module 2, The Importance of Language
- additional reading, 80
- agenda, *78, 79, 81*
- child development topics in, *79,* 79–80
- closing, *81*
- conflict and conflict resolution investigations in, 81, *81*
- content and process purposes of, *152*
- facilitator role, *78, 79, 81*
- goals of, 77, 78
- investigator role, *78, 79, 81*
- learning process, *78, 79, 81*
- mental models, 78
- nine language concepts, 77, 78
- *See also* Modules

Module 3, Theory of Change
- agenda, *84, 89*
- closing, *89*
- content and process purposes of, *152*
- creating mental model in, 85–87, *88*
- facilitator role, *84, 89*
- goals, 83
- group development and, 9
- investigator discomfort in exploration of, 85–86
- investigator role, *84, 89*
- learning process, *84, 89*
- Stages of Change discussion in, 89
- use of Mental Model of Process of Change, 85
- *See also* Modules

Module 4, The Rich/Poor Gap and Research on Causes of Poverty
- agenda, *92, 93, 95, 102, 105*
- CEO Pay Gap Activity in, 98–99
- closing, *105*
- content and process purposes of, *153*
- creating Mental Models of Wealth and Middle Class in, *102,* 103–104
- facilitator role, *91*–*92, 92, 93, 95, 102, 105*
- goals, 92
- Income Quintiles Activity in, 96–97
- investigation of community conditions, 93
- investigation of individual behaviors and choices, 93
- investigation of predatory practices, 94
- investigator role, *92, 93, 95, 102, 105*
- learning process, *92, 93, 95, 102, 105*
- managing discussion in, 93
- reading list, 92
- Ten Chairs Activity in, 100–101
- *See also* Modules

Module 5, Hidden Rules of Economic Class
- agenda, *108, 110, 113, 115*
- closing, *115*
- content and process purposes of, *153*
- facilitator role, *108, 110,* 110–112, *113, 115*
- goals of, 107, 112–113
- investigator role, *108, 110, 113, 115*
- learning process, *108, 110, 113, 115*
- Time-Management Matrix in, *115*
- *See also* Modules

Module 6, Eleven Resources
- agenda, *118–119*
- assessing case studies in, *119,* 120
- content and process purposes of, *153*
- facilitator role, *118–119,* 120
- goals of, 119
- investigator role, *118–119*
- learning process, *118–119*
- *See also* Modules

Module 7, Threat Assessment, 121, *122*
    content and process purposes of, *153*
    See also Modules
Module 8, Self-Assessment of Resources
    agenda, *124*
    closing, *124*
    content and process purposes of, 123, *125*, *153*
    facilitator role, *124*, 125
    investigator role, *124*
    See also Modules
Module 9, Community Assessment, 70, 93
    agenda, *128, 130*
    closing, *130*
    content and process purposes of, 127, *154*
    facilitator role, *128, 130*
    goals of, 127
    information gathering for, 129
    investigator role, *128, 130*
    learning process, *128, 130*
    mental models for, 127, 129
    See also Modules
Module 10, Building Resources, 133–135
    content and process purposes of, *154*
    See also Modules
Module 11, Personal and Community Plans
    agenda, *138–139*
    closing, *139*
    content and process purposes of, 137, *154*
    creating SMART Plan in, 140
    facilitator role, *138–139*
    investigator role, *138–139*
    learning process, *138–139*
    See also Modules
Modules
    content knowledge of, 151
    learning process, 70, 151
    patterns in, 69–70
    purpose of, 8
    schedule, *59*
    sequence and reinforcement of key concepts, 142
    sequence for hidden rules of class investigation, *143–144*
    sequence for income and wealth disparity investigation, *143–144*
    sequence for investigating effects of change on relationships, *147–148*
    sequence for investigating motivation, 149
    sequence for investigating relationships, 150
    sequence for theory of change investigation, *145–146*
    workbook section headings, 70
    See also specific modules (1–11), above
Motivation, 13, 58, 149
Motivational Interviewing: Preparing People for Change (Miller & Rollnick), 13
Moustakas, C., 63
Mozilo, A., 99
MPOWR, 28, *32*, 125, 160
My Economic Class Story, *105*
My Family Structure, Mental Model of, *113*
My Future Story Mental Model, *139*, 140
My Life upon Release, 73, 89, 140
My Threat Assessment, *122*

N

Narrative Therapy: The Social Construction of Preferred Realities (Freedman & Combs), 9
Needs-based models, 48–49, 51
Negotiations, 81, *81*

O

Offenders
    defined, 162
    working with, 56–57
One-on-One Relationships Mental Model, 127, *130*, 131
Orientation, 19–20

P

Participatory discourse, 69
Payday lending, 94
Payne, R., 2, 45, 63
Pedagogy of the Oppressed (Freire), 2, 13
Personal story, *6, 8*
Planning and problem solving
    in Getting Out Reentry Model, 23
    role of returning citizens in, 1, 2, 21
    skills of under-resourced people, 3
    See also Problem solvers, investigators as
Planning backwards, 119
Planning backward exercise, *138, 146*
Poverty
    Bridges Continuum approach to, 35, *36–37*
    causes of, 2, 3, 91, *92*
    change in relationships in transition from, 109
    community sustainability and, 157

defined, 117, *118,* 120
effects of, 2
facilitators' and sponsors' understanding of, 1
failure of programs to reduce, 2
in Getting Ahead philosophy, 2, 91
institutional and community outcomes of, 4
investigator's self-awareness of near-poverty status, 15
mental model of, 9, 10, *72, 73,* 73–74, 129
needs-based approach for alleviating, 48–49
obstacles to moving out of, 3
political salience of, 91
problem-solving skills of people in, 3, 103–104
resources in maintenance of, 48–49
systemic factors in, 119
See also Module 4, The Rich/Poor Gap and Research on Causes of Poverty

Power
economic class and, *102,* 103
hidden rules of economic class and, 16, 111
public policy and, *110*
responsibility and, 16
sources of, 16

Power-based models, 49, 51
Power of TED, The (Emerald), 57
Preceptors, 65
Predatory practices, *93,* 94
Pre/Post Assessment, 28, 29, 160
Problem solvers, investigators as, 2, 3, *12,* 20, 22, 23, 53, 103–104, 131
Prowell, J., 13–15
Putnam, R., 42

Q

Quality-of-life indicators, 157–158
Questioning techniques, 61–62

R

Racism and discrimination, 14–15
Rankism, 55
Recidivism
defined, 162
facilitators' and sponsors' understanding of, 1
failure of programs to reduce, 2
goals of Reentry Model, 2
personal relationships and, 109
risk of, three years after return, x
threat assessment to prevent, *122*
Recordkeeping, 21

Recruitment, 19
Reentry Model
challenges in implementing, xi
community role in, 27
component plans, 162
comprehensive approach of, 23
cooperation with existing reentry programs, 24, 27–28
core constructs, 23
cornerstone of, 16
data collection tools for, 28–32
data-driven approach of, 23
download, 22
expected outcomes, 2
family member participation in, 26
flexibility of, 23
frequently asked questions, 25–28
goals of, 22
Model Fidelity checklist, 21
origins and development of, ix–x, 22
philosophical basis of, 2–4
principles of, 23–24
requirements for successful implementation of, x
resources for implementation, 23–24
role of correctional facility in implementation of, 26
sequenced implementation, 26
sharing among sites using, 25
sponsors, 25
start-up, 26
steps in implementation of, 25
support from Bridges initiatives for, ix–x, 22, 23, 26, 33, 57
See also Getting Ahead while Getting Out; Modules; *specific module*
Reflective listening, 62
Registers of language, 7, 11, 53, 54, 62, 64, *78,* 111
Reinforcement, 8, 142
Reintegration, 162
Relational learning, 63
Research Continuum, *12,* 91, 92, 93
Resources
assessment of, 3
building, 133–135
for change, 13
defining and identifying, *118–119,* 120
in definition of poverty, 117, 120
to facilitate abstract thinking, 9
for Getting Ahead graduates, 47–48

getting-by versus getting-ahead, 48–51, *50, 134,* 135
goals of Getting Ahead, 4
hidden rules of economic class and, 111
for implementing Getting Out Reentry Model, 23–24
mental model of, *124*
organizational collaboration to build, 51
in power-based models, 49, 51
self-assessment of, 123–125, *153*
for solving concrete problems, 87
stability and, 43
See also Module 6, Eleven Resources
Resources Development Plan, 162, 163
Responsibility, 16
Restored citizen, 163
Returning citizens
    challenges in finding motivation for change, 13
    changed relationships of, 109
    considerations in working with, 57
    defined, 163
    goals of Getting Ahead program for, ix
    mobile app to support, 31
    planning and problem solving by, 1, 2, 3, 21
    resources for families of, 24
    risk of reoffending by, after three years, x
    72-Hour Stability Plan for, 57, 121, *122, 138,* 162
    See also Support for graduates of Bridges and Getting Ahead programs
Return on investment, 23
Rich Dad, Poor Dad (Kiyosaki), 111
Right-handed conversations, 60
"Righting reflex," 6, 33, 62, *84*
Risley, T. R., 80
Rituals, 60
Rogers, C., 13
Rollnick, S., 13
Ross, C., *89*
R Rules, 26, *119*
R Rules, The (Souther), 24, 35, *119*

S

Schedule, meeting, 20, *59*
Schwartz, P., *85*
Section 8 housing, 48
Self-assessment
    awareness of near-poverty status, 15
    facilitator's, 55
    hidden rules of economic class and, 112
    of resources, 3, 123–125
    for 72-Hour Stability Plan, 121
Self-image, *43*
Senge, P., 10
Separating problem from person, 3, 8–9, 54, 61, 86
72-Hour Stability Plan, 57, 121, *122, 138,* 162
Shaull, R., 2
Short-termism, 4
SMART Plan, 24, 58, *138,* 140, 163
Sober living houses, 163
Social capital
    bonding vs. bridging, 109
    building, 57
    capacity for abstract thinking and, 87
    formal and informal, 42
    in Getting Ahead philosophy, 4
    goals of co-investigation, 7
    mental model of, *118,* 150
    significance of, in Bridges initiatives, 47
    See also Support for graduates of Bridges and Getting Ahead programs
Source, The (MI), 45
South Bend (IN) Future Story Project, 45
Souther, B., 24, 35
Sowell, T., 157
Sponsors
    agendas of, and agenda-free approach of Getting Ahead, 34–35
    in co-investigation, 1
    of Getting Out Reentry Model, 25
    preparation for implementing Reentry Model, x
    resources for implementing Reentry Model, 24
St. Joseph County (IN) Bridges Out of Poverty Initiative, 28, 29, 44, 160, 161
Stability
    environmental, continuum of, *5*
    resource building and, 43
Stability Plan, 24
Stability Scale, *84*
Stages of Change, 60, 89, *89*
Story lines, *6,* 8
Supplemental Security Income, 48
Supply Core, Inc., 160
SupplyCore Technology Group, 125
Support for Change Mental Model, *139*
Support for graduates of Bridges and Getting Ahead programs
    challenges, 39
    community models of, 44

from corporate and business sector, 45
from criminal justice sector, 47
determinants of quality of, 42
development of learning community for, 40–42
from fellow investigators, 42
financial, 51
formal and informal, 42
in health sector, 47
local conditions as factor in provision of, 42
in postsecondary sector, 45–46
preparation for, in program design, 42
from program graduates, 67
resource building for, 47–48
sources of, 42, 47
unique features of Bridges Model for, *40–41*
Sutton, S., *55*

T

Tactical Communication, 24
Taylor, C., 48, *110, 135*
Taylor-Ide, D., *48, 110, 135*
Temporary Assistance to Needy Families (TANF), 48
Ten Chairs Activity, The, 100–101
Theory of change
    in Getting Ahead philosophy, 3
    module sequence for investigation of, *145–146*
    See also Module 3, Theory of Change
Time
    changes in use of, for Getting Ahead graduates, *43*
    hidden rule for, 111–112
    management and planning, 58
Time-Management Matrix, *115*
Tinto, V., *46*
Training
    for community volunteers, 26, 27
    for correctional staff, 26
    facilitator, 20, 24, 25, 26–27
    for graduate support, 42
    for implementing Reentry Model, 25
Transitional control, 163
Treatment "in lieu of," 4, 163
Triangle (Process), 8, 54, 71
Trust, 15, *15,* 19, 150
Tyranny of the moment, 2, 3, 4, 9, 87, 104
    hidden rule for time and, 111–112

U

Understanding and Engaging Under-Resourced College Students, 45
Unequal Childhoods: Class, Race, and Family Life (Lareau), 80
United for a Fair Economy (UFE), *95,* 99, 161

V

Vella, J., 8, 58
Vocabulary, 11

W

Wage gap, 98–99
Wall, J., 5
Watson, L., 14, *67*
Wealth
    income versus, 100–101
    mental model of, *102,* 103–104
    power and, *102,* 103
Wealthy class
    in Getting Ahead partnerships, 4
    time for abstract pursuits among, 4
"Welfare," 80
Wheatley, M., 10
Whole Foods Market, 99
Women, Infants, and Children, 49
Wood, M., ix
Working Bridges (VT), 45

Y

Youngstown (OH) State University Bridges Out of Poverty Student Union, 42, *44,* 47

About the Authors

Philip E. "Phil" DeVol, Marengo, OH, president and CEO of DeVol & Associates, LLC, has been training and consulting on poverty issues since 1997. He co-authored *Bridges Out of Poverty: Strategies for Professionals and Communities* (1999) with Ruby K. Payne, PhD, and Terie Dreussi-Smith, and in 2004 he wrote the first edition of *Getting Ahead in a Just-Gettin'-By World: Building Your Resources for a Better Life* to help people in poverty investigate the impact of poverty on their communities and themselves.

He works in North America and internationally with communities that apply Bridges Constructs, including sites in Canada, Australia, and Slovakia (where Bridges Communities have been awarded two European Union grants to further the work there). Bridges Communities bring people together from all classes, political persuasions, and sectors to address all causes of poverty in a systemic way. The many Bridges Communities using Getting Ahead led to this new edition of Getting Ahead titled *Getting Ahead while Getting Out*.

DeVol consults with Bridges Communities on a variety of topics to assist knowledge transfer among the many individuals, organizations, and communities that are adopting Bridges principles in their settings, as well as developing new levels of expertise. In addition to writing and consulting, DeVol works with aha! Process's collaborations with other organizations to implement innovative, high-impact strategies for ending poverty and building sustainable communities where everyone can do well.

His 2010 workbook and facilitator guide *Investigations into Economic Class in America,* co-authored with Karla M. Krodel, applies the Getting Ahead concepts to college life for under-resourced postsecondary students. That book was honored in 2011 by the Association of Educational Publishers, winning its Distinguished Achievement Award for Adult Curriculum (Life Skills); the book was also a 2011 Innovation Award finalist. Finally, a collection of DeVol's essays and articles was published in 2010 under the title *Bridges to Sustainable Communities: A Systemwide, Cradle-to-Grave Approach to Ending Poverty in America,* describes how communities, organizations, and businesses across the U.S. have applied Bridges concepts.

In his current work DeVol builds on his 19 years as director of an Ohio outpatient substance abuse treatment facility in which he designed treatment programs and collaborative systems for school-based prevention, community-based intervention, and Ohio's first alternative school for recovering young people. During this time he also co-authored *The Complete Guide to Elementary Student Assistance Programs* (1993) with Linda Christensen.

He and his wife, Susan, live in rural Ohio just a few miles from his two children and three grandchildren.

Michelle R. Wood, Marion, OH, licensed social worker (LSW), is a probation officer with the Marion County Adult Probation Department.

She has been part of the Getting Ahead program and the Bridges Out of Poverty initiative for five years. She serves as co-chairperson on the Mid-Ohio Reentry Committee and is a member of the Marion County Common Pleas Court's Reentry Advisory Committee. She is vice president of the Marion Matters Board of Directors and is co-chairperson of Marion Matters Felony Assistance Team.

From the time Michelle was 10 years old she was in and out of the juvenile judicial system. When she became an adult, she served three years in the Ohio Reformatory for Women. Upon her release, she dealt with the same barriers that most returning citizens encounter. Wood has worked hard to change her life and has a passion for helping others make a successful return to their community.

She has two sons and enjoys traveling around Ohio to watch them compete in sports activities.

Mitchell A. "Mitch" Libster, Marion, OH, worked as the managing attorney of the Marion Branch of the Legal Aid Society of Marion for 33 years, retiring in 2013. He has been involved with many community activities, including the Boys and Girls Club of Marion, the Marion Metropolitan Housing Authority, and the Board of Trustees of Marion Technical College. He also served on the Marion County Children Services Board and is currently on the Facility Governing Board of the West Central Community Correctional Facility in Marysville, OH.

Libster has facilitated five series of Getting Ahead classes in Marion and three at the Reintegration Camp of the Marion Correctional Institution. His interests include running, gardening, playing bridge, and spending time with his grandchildren.

He and his wife, Cindy, have four children and seven grandchildren, all of whom live in the Columbus, OH, area.

More eye-openers at ... www.ahaprocess.com

- Visit www.ahaprocess.com for free resources: articles, video clips, success stories from practitioners, and read our blog!
  - Sign up for our latest workshop offerings (many online), including:
  - Getting Ahead while Getting Out Facilitator Certification
  - Getting Ahead in a Just-Gettin'-By World Facilitator Training
  - Bridges to Health and Healthcare
  - Applying Bridges Concepts: Individual and Institutional
  - Bridges Out of Poverty Trainer Certification
  - Building a Sustainable Community
  - Understanding Class for First Responders

- Visit www.gettingaheadnetwork.com for more information on community-based models that will work where you live

- If you like *Getting Ahead while Getting Out,* check out:
  - *Bridges to Health and Healthcare: New solutions for improving access and services* (Payne, Dreussi-Smith, Shaw, & Young)
  - *From Vision to Action, Vol. II: Best Practices to reduce the impact of poverty in communities, education, healthcare, and more* (peer-reviewed articles written by practitioners of the work)
  - *Investigations into Economic Class in America & Facilitator Notes* (DeVol & Krodel). This is Getting Ahead adapted for college students
  - *Bridges to Sustainable Communities: A Systemwide, Cradle-to-Grave Approach to Ending Poverty in America* (DeVol) for techniques, training, and tips for generating Bridges Communities
  - *Tactical Communication: Mastering effective interactions with citizens of diverse backgrounds* (Pfarr)

- Connect with us on FaceBook, Twitter, and Pinterest, and watch our YouTube channel

For a complete listing of products, please visit www.ahaprocess.com

Join us on Facebook
www.facebook.com/rubypayne
www.facebook.com/bridgesoutofpoverty
www.facebook.com/ahaprocess
www.facebook.com/CollegeAchievementAlliance

Twitter
www.twitter.com/ahaprocess
@ahaprocess

Pinterest
http://www.pinterest.com/ahaprocess/

Subscribe to our YouTube channel
www.youtube.com/ahaprocess

Respond to our blog
www.ahaprocess.com/blog

Download free resources
www.ahaprocess.com